T TO

TONY HOLMES

D1440135

First published in Great Britain in 2007 by Osprey Publishing,
Midland House, West Way, Botley, Oxford OX2 0PH, UK

443 Park Avenue South, New York, NY 10016, USA

E-mail: info@ospreypublishing.com

A CIP catalogue record for this book is available from the British Library

ISBN: 978 1 84603 190 8

Page layout by Myriam Bell
Index by Alan Thatcher
Battlescene by Mark Postlethwaite
Typeset in ITC Conduit and Adobe Garamond
Maps by Bounford
Originated by PDQ Digital Media Solutions
Printed in China through Bookbuilders

08 09 10 11 12 11 10 9 8 7 6 5 4 3 2

For a catalogue of all books published by Osprey Military and Aviation please contact:

NORTH AMERICA
Osprey Direct, c/o Random House Distribution Center, 400 Hahn Road, Westminster, MD
21157

E-mail: info@ospreydirect.com

ALL OTHER REGIONS
Osprey Direct UK, P.O. Box 140 Wellingborough, Northants, NN8 2FA, UK

E-mail: info@ospreydirect.co.uk

www.ospreypublishing.com

Acknowledgements:

Photographs have been supplied from the archives of Peter Arnold, Eddie Creek, Philip
Jarrett, Wojtek Matusiak, Dr Alfred Price, Jerry Scutts, Andrew Thomas and John Weal.

Editor's note:

For ease of comparison, imperial measurements are used
almost exclusively throughout this book. The exception is
weapons calibres, which are given in their official
designation, whether metric or imperial. The following list
will help in converting the imperial measurements to
metric:

1 mile = 1.6km
1lb = 0.45kg
1 yard = 0.9m
1ft = 0.3m
1in. = 2.54cm
1 gal = 4.5 litres

Spitfire cover art

Plt Off Bob Doe of No. 234 Sqn, flying his Spitfire IA
X4036, keeps a watchful eye on a second Bf 109E shortly
after claiming his 11th victory of the Battle of Britain, and
the fifth Bf 109E he had destroyed in three days. Bob Doe
routinely hunted German aircraft along the Kent coast
near Dover following bombing raids on London, as he
recalled in his autobiography *Fighter Pilot*. 'I assumed that
enemy aircraft would be crossing the coast at about
10,000–12,000ft in a gentle dive, heading for home – and
trade should be brisk, as they would be thinking of home,
more than Spitfires.'

Bf 109E cover art

Having been made Gruppenkommandeur of I./JG 52 on
28 August 1940, future 77-victory *experte* Hauptmann
Wolfgang Ewald celebrated his promotion five days later
when he was one of three pilots from the Gruppe each to
claim a Spitfire destroyed. The latter were almost certainly
from Croydon-based No. 72 Sqn, which was attacked
whilst patrolling over Lympne, in Kent.
(Cover artwork by Jim Laurier)

German ranks	RAF equivalent
Reichsmarschall	no equivalent
Generalfeldmarschall	Marshal of the Royal Air Force
Generaloberst	Air Chief Marshal
General der Flieger	Air Marshal
Generalleutnant	Air Vice Marshal
Generalmajor	Air Commodore
Oberst	Group Captain
Oberstleutnant (Obstlt)	Wing Commander
Major	Squadron Leader
Hauptmann (Hptm)	Flight Lieutenant
Oberleutnant (Oblt)	Flying Officer
Leutnant (Ltn)	Pilot Officer
Stabsfeldwebel (StFw)	Warrant Officer
Oberfeldwebel (Ofw)	Flight Sergeant
Fähnrich (Fhr)	Officer candidate
Feldwebel (Fw)	Sergeant
Unteroffizier (Uffz)	Corporal
Obergefreiter (Ogfr)	Leading Aircraftman
Gefreiter (Gefr)	Aircraftman First Class
Flieger (Flg)	Aircraftman Second Class

CONTENTS

INTRODUCTION

Fighter-versus-fighter combat has always held a particular fascination for historians and aviation enthusiasts alike, and perhaps the ultimate aerial joust of the 20th century took place over the skies of southern England during the long, hot summer of 1940. The fate of the free world effectively rested on the shoulders of several thousand aviators (supported by thousands more groundcrew, radar plotters, fighter controllers and observers) who flew with RAF Fighter Command in direct defence of the British Isles. Their opponents, the battle-hardened Luftwaffe, had been given the job of neutralizing Britain's aerial defences so that a seaborne invasion could be launched across the Channel from occupied France. At the forefront of the action were 19 Spitfire squadrons, charged with defending their more numerous Hurricane brethren from attack by Bf 109s as the Hawker fighters attempted to repel the hordes of medium bombers dispatched by the Luftwaffe to knock out key industrial and military targets.

The remarkable similarities in terms of performance between the Bf 109E and the Spitfire I/II, the predominant models used by the rival air forces, are highlighted in this volume. Both were the product of several years' development during the 1930s as Britain and Germany rapidly re-armed, and they were the most advanced fighter types in frontline service in 1940. By examining the strengths and weaknesses of both aircraft, the technical nuances of each fighter are revealed, as is the reality of using the fighters within a combat situation. With both aircraft being so evenly matched, the battle really came down to the skill of the pilots involved, and their employment of superior tactics, to ensure victory. The Spitfire and Bf 109E had initially met over the evacuation beaches of Dunkirk in the final days of May 1940, and neither fighter managed to gain a clear advantage over the other. The German fighter pilots, near exhaustion and at the end of an overstretched supply chain

following the rapid advances of the Blitzkrieg through the Low Countries of Western Europe, were flying their favoured freelance sweeps into the areas patrolled by RAF Fighter Command. The British units were also experiencing operational difficulties of their own as their 'short-legged' fighters were operating at the extreme limits of their range.

Nevertheless, Spitfire and Bf 109E pilots that survived the bloody clashes over the French coast, gained a valuable insight into the strengths and weaknesses of their much vaunted opponents. Fighter Command's tactics were quickly exposed as being terribly out of date, and therefore dangerous to those pilots ordered to adhere to them during the summer of 1940. The Spitfire more than held its own in combat with Europe's all-conquering fighter, however, and the majority of RAF pilots serving in the frontline felt confident that they could prevail over the Bf 109E when engaged by the Germans over home territory.

The Jagdwaffe, in turn, was anxious to exploit the apparent weakness in British fighter tactics, and the more senior pilots in the German Bf 109E ranks were also quietly confident that they could defeat even the most aggressively flown Spitfire. They were fully aware that the Messerschmitt fighter's endurance could pose problems, but they believed their preferred – and combat tested – slashing tactics, which meant that the Jagdflieger attacked with deadly accuracy from high altitude and then headed straight home, would alleviate any range issues.

Eager to fight each other for the mastery of the skies over southern England, Spitfire and Bf 109E pilots prepared themselves for possibly the most important aerial clash of World War II – the Battle of Britain.

Spitfire I/IIs and Bf 109Es were rarely seen together in close proximity on the ground in 1940. However, on a handful of occasions that year RAF pilots flying damaged aircraft were forced down in France, as seen here. No. 603 'City of Edinburgh' Sqn Spitfire IA X4260, flown by Plt Off Bill Caister, was damaged in combat over the Channel near Manston by future 77-victory ace Hauptmann Hubertus von Bonin of I./JG 54. Caister force-landed in a field near Guines, in northern France, and the Spitfire was eventually sent to Germany for full flight evaluation, being flown at Augsburg by famous Messerschmitt test pilot Fritz Wendel.

CHRONOLOGY

1933

6 July   Reichsluftfahrtministerium (RLM) issues Tactical Requirements for Fighter Aircraft (Land). The Bf 109 is one of four designs put forward.

1934

February   R. J. Mitchell's first fighter design, the Vickers Supermarine Type 224, powered by a Rolls-Royce Goshawk, makes its maiden flight.

March   Design work commences on the Bf 109.

1 Dec   Air Ministry issues a contract to Vickers Supermarine for the new Mitchell-designed, Rolls-Royce PV 12 Merlin-powered monoplane fighter, writing Specification F37/34 around it.

1935

28 May   Rolls-Royce Kestrel-powered Bf 109 V1 prototype performs its maiden flight.

1936

January   Junkers Jumo 210-powered Bf 109 V2 joins the flight trial programme, where both prototypes are flown alongside the rival Heinkel He 112 fighter.

5 March   Prototype Type 300 K5054 (later christened 'Spitfire'), powered by a Rolls-Royce Merlin C driving a two-bladed fixed pitch de Havilland. propeller, makes its maiden flight from Eastleigh airfield, near Southampton.

June   Vickers Supermarine signs a contract with the Air Ministry to produce 310 Spitfire I aircraft.

Autumn   Following a series of exhaustive trials, the Bf 109 is chosen for production ahead of the He 112 due to its being faster and more manoeuvrable.

Spitfire IIA fuselages are mass produced at the Nuffield Shadow Factory at Castle Bromwich, near Birmingham, in late 1940.

1937

February   First of 344 Bf 109Bs leave the Augsburg factory and are issued to II./JG 132 'Richthofen'.

June   Bf 109 V10 fitted with a Daimler-Benz DB 600Aa engine.

1938

Spring   Bf 109C, fitted with fuel-injected Jumo 210Ga engine and wing-mounted machine guns, enters production. Bf 109D, powered by the Jumo 210Da engine with a carburettor, also enters production at this time.

14 May   First production Spitfire I makes its maiden flight one year later than planned due to a shortage of skilled labour and manufacturing difficulties.

August   No. 19 Sqn at Duxford becomes the first unit in RAF Fighter Command to be issued with Spitfires.

December   First production Bf 109E-1s, fitted with the definitive fuel-injected Daimler-Benz DB 601 engine, enter frontline service. More than 4,000 Bf 109Es would eventually be built.

1939

1 Sep	German troops invade Poland, and Bf 109Cs from I./JG 21 claim five PZL P.24 fighters destroyed as the fighter's first victories of World War II.
16 Oct	No. 603 Sqn shoots down a Ju 88 bomber over the Firth of Forth for the Spitfire I's first victory.

1940

23 May	Spitfire Is and Bf 109Es clash for the first time when Nos 74 and 54 Sqns tangle with I./JG 27 near the Dunkirk evacuation beaches.
Summer	Improved Bf 109E-3/4s begin to enter service, fitted with more armoured protection and twin MG FF 20mm cannon in the wings.
June	Production of the Spitfire II at the Nuffield factory in Castle Bromwich commences, with the first examples reaching No. 611 Sqn in July.
June	Hispano 20mm cannon-armed Spitfire IB enters service with No. 19 Sqn.

This Bf 109E-3 was assigned to Oberleutnant Werner Pichon-Kalau von Hofe, technical officer of III./JG 51, in the early summer of 1940. Von Hofe claimed six victories (including three Spitfires) during the Battle of Britain.

10 July	Battle of Britain officially commences, with 348 Spitfire Is split between 19 squadrons in RAF Fighter Command opposing eight *Jagdgeschwader* (fighter wings) equipped with 809 Bf 109Es.
August	Bf 109E-7, derived from the DB 601N-powered E-4/N, and capable of carrying a drop tank or bombs, enters service.
13 August	*Adlertag* (Eagle Day): Luftwaffe launches all-out offensive against RAF but loses 45 aeroplanes to the RAF's 13.
15 Sep	One of the heaviest bombing raids by the Luftwaffe, today celebrated as Battle of Britain Day.
October	First examples of the Bf 109F are issued to JG 51.
31 Oct	Battle of Britain officially ends, with Spitfire units having downed 521 German aircraft and Fighter Command having lost 403 Spitfires in combat. Some 610 Bf 109Es had been destroyed in action between 10 July and 31 October.
Autumn	Bomb-equipped Bf 109E-7s commence *Jabo* (a contraction of *Jagdbomber* – fighter-bomber) operations over south-east England.

1941

10 Jan	First official 'Circus' offensive mission into Europe includes three squadrons of Spitfires.
Spring	Bf 109Es steadily replaced on the Channel front by the Bf 109F. Spitfire IIA (long range) fighters, equipped with 40-gal (Imperial) fixed tank under port wing, commence operations over France.
Autumn	Last examples of Bf 109E in the west soldier on with JG 1 and JG 2.

1942

January	Last Spitfire IIs in Fighter Command retired by No. 152 Sqn.

DESIGN AND DEVELOPMENT

SPITFIRE

Vickers Supermarine, the manufacturer of one of history's greatest aircraft, in fact had little experience of building fighter aircraft prior to placing the Spitfire into production. It had, however, been heavily involved in high-performance aviation through its family of flying-boat and floatplane racers of the 1920s and early 1930s.

Based in Woolston, Southampton, the company, and its chief designer, Reginald J. Mitchell, initially achieved prominence internationally when Supermarine's Sea Lion biplane won the Schneider Trophy in 1922. Over the next nine years the company would secure further racing successes, and set world speed records, with its S 4, S 5, S 6 and S 6B floatplanes. A fruitful relationship with Rolls-Royce's aero engine division was also cultivated during this period.

Vickers Aviation acquired a majority shareholding in Supermarine in 1928, and this helped the company survive the lean inter-war period when few military orders were on offer. Indeed, the bulk of Supermarine's work during this time centred on the construction of 79 Southampton flying-boats for the RAF.

In 1931 the Air Ministry issued Specification F7/30 for a new fighter for frontline service with the RAF that would boast a higher top speed than the 225mph Bristol Bulldog – little more than half the speed of the S 6B Schneider Trophy winner! The winning design would also have to be armed with four 0.303-in. machine guns, which was double the armament of the RAF's biplane fighters then in squadron service.

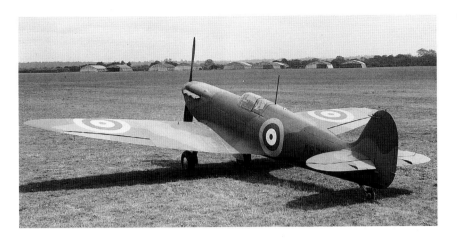

The very first production Spitfire I built, K9787 made its maiden flight on 5 May 1938 – a full 26 months after the prototype K5054 had taken to the skies for the first time. Used extensively by Supermarine as a trials and test-bed aircraft, K9787 was eventually stripped of its armament and converted into a photo-reconnaissance platform in the spring of 1941, but was lost later that year.

Because military orders were scarce for the British aviation industry at the time the F7/30 specification was issued, no fewer than eight manufacturers produced prototypes in response. Supermarine's 660hp Rolls-Royce Goshawk-powered Type 224 was one of three monoplane prototypes put forward. The Goshawk used the newly developed evaporative-cooling system rather than conventional external radiators, which meant that the aircraft could feature cleaner aerodynamics. The Type 224, with its distinctive low-mounted cranked wing and fixed 'trousered' undercarriage, made its first flight in February 1934, and the combination of evaporative cooling and the low-wing monoplane design soon presented Supermarine with serious engine overheating problems. The aircraft's performance was also disappointing, with a top speed of just 238mph due to its overly thick wing and fixed undercarriage. It came as no surprise, therefore, that Gloster's SS 37 biplane, which was marginally faster and considerably more manoeuvrable, was chosen as the winner. Developed from the company's successful Gauntlet biplane, the new fighter would enter service with the RAF as the Gladiator – Britain's last biplane fighter.

Undaunted by this initial failure, Mitchell and his team started work on a far cleaner airframe that would feature a retractable undercarriage and a considerably more powerful engine. The latter had emerged from Rolls-Royce in late 1934 in the form of the PV 12 (later renamed the Merlin). The company rated the engine at 790hp when unveiled, but the manufacturer hoped to eventually get 1,000hp from it. By this time Mitchell was already seriously ill with cancer. In 1933 he had taken a holiday to Europe to convalesce from an operation, and had met with some German aviators. He became convinced that war was inevitable and was determined to make his contribution by providing the design for a battle-winning fighter.

At the same time Vickers allocated funds for Mitchell and his team to proceed with their PV 12-powered fighter, which was designated the Supermarine Type 300. Although initially started as a private venture at Woolston, the Air Ministry quickly became interested in the aircraft. On 1 December 1934 it issued a contract worth £10,000 to Supermarine for construction of a prototype to Mitchell's 'improved F7/30' design, the new fighter receiving the designation F37/34.

OPPOSITE
Assigned to Plt Off Bob Doe,
X4036 was also used by
leading No. 234 Sqn ace Flg
Off Paterson Hughes. Indeed,
the Australian claimed two
Bf 109Es from 1./JG 27
destroyed off the Isle of
Wight on the afternoon of
18 August 1940 whilst flying
this machine.

The new Rolls-Royce engine was a third larger, both in terms of its weight and size in comparison with the Goshawk, so in order to compensate for the forward shift in the centre of gravity the sweepback of the leading edge of the fighter's wing was reduced. Soon, the wing had taken on an elliptical shape, as aerodynamicists at Supermarine calculated that it would create the lowest induced drag in flight. Such a flying surface also meant that the wing root would be thick enough to house the undercarriage when retracted.

Beverley Shenstone, the aerodynamicist on the Type 300 team, told noted aviation historian Dr Alfred Price that:

> I remember once discussing the shape with R J Mitchell, and he said jokingly 'I don't give a bugger whether it's elliptical or not, so long as it covers the guns!' The ellipse was simply the shape that allowed us the thinnest possible wing with sufficient room inside to carry the necessary structure and the things we wanted to cram in.

Mitchell's mentioning of the guns in this quote reflects the fact that in April 1935 Supermarine was asked by the Operational Requirements section of the Air Ministry to double the firepower being installed into the wings of its new fighter by fitting eight rather than four 0.303-in. Browning machine guns. Each gun would have its own 300-round ammunition box.

One of the final problems overcome with the prototype Type 300 prior to the aircraft being rolled out for the first time centred on the cooling for the PV 12 engine. Rolls-Royce had hoped to use the evaporative system once again, but this had performed so badly in the Type 224 that Mitchell was forced to go with an external radiator, and the drag it produced. However, a newly-developed ducted radiator designed by Fred Meredith of the Royal Aircraft Establishment (RAE) promised to offset the drag through its ability to expel compressed, heated air at increased velocity through a divergent duct. Thus, when the prototype F37/34 was rolled out of the Woolston works on the banks of the River Itchen for the first time in February 1936, it boasted a Meredith-type ducted radiator beneath its starboard wing.

Following a series of ground runs, the fighter was dismantled and trucked to Supermarine's airfield at nearby Eastleigh. Once reassembled and passed fit to fly by the Aeronautical Inspection Directorate, the unpainted Type 300, wearing the serial K5054 and RAF roundels, took to the skies at 1630hrs. At the controls was Vickers' chief test pilot, Capt Joseph 'Mutt' Summers, who was aloft for just eight minutes.

By early April the initial test programme had been completed, and on 26 May the prototype was delivered to the RAF trials establishment at Martlesham Heath. After a brief series of early flights had revealed the fighter's potential (including possessing a top speed of 349mph), the Air Ministry signed a contract with Vickers Supermarine for 310 fighters. There was some debate over what the new fighter should be called. According to the historian Robert Bungay, Vickers appeared to think of aeroplanes as 'bad tempered women'. They had previously come up with 'Shrew' but Mitchell apparently objected to this denigration of his elegant design and was overheard to remark caustically that it was 'just the sort of silly name they would give it'.

SPITFIRE IA OF NO. 603 SQN

29ft 11in.

12ft 7.75in.

36ft 10in.

The eventual name actually came from the Vickers' Chairman, Sir Robert Maclean, who called his daughter 'a little Spitfire', and it was approved by the Air Ministry.

As the sole prototype, K5054 was progressively modified into a more representative frontline fighter. For example, in August 1936 the aircraft returned to Eastleigh for the installation of eight 0.303-in. machine guns, a reflector gunsight and radio. Ever more powerful versions of the Merlin engine were also fitted during 1936 and 1937.

On 11 June 1937, with K5054 still the only airworthy example of the Spitfire in existence, its creator, Reginald J. Mitchell, succumbed to cancer at the age of just 42, having dedicated his health and the final years of his life to creating the aeroplane. In the wake of his death, Supermarine's chief draughtsman Joe Smith was promoted to chief designer, and he took charge of the Spitfire's development.

One of the more persistent problems facing Smith and his team was the freezing of the machine guns in the wings when the aircraft climbed up to 32,000ft. This issue first arose in March 1937, and it was not effectively cured until October of the following year – the ducting of hot air from the underwing radiator eventually cured the problem. By then the first production aircraft had at last reached Fighter Command, some 12 months later than scheduled.

The stressed-skin structure of the hand-finished prototype had proven difficult to replicate when it came to building production aircraft in jigs. The aircraft's elliptical wings could not be built using existing production techniques, and being all-metal, they were hard to make and hard to repair. Progress to this point had also been slowed by the redrafting of the prototype drawings so that they could be used as blueprints from which to build combat-capable Spitfires – this took a year to complete. Once it came time to cut, forge or cast metal, Supermarine encountered further problems employing sufficiently skilled workers to man its production line.

Mitchell had sacrificed everything for performance, and as a result, a Spitfire took two-and-a-half times as long to build as a Hurricane and twice as long as a

The first RAF unit to receive Spitfire Is was No. 19 Sqn, which began replacing its Gauntlets with Supermarine fighters from August 1938. Based at RAF Duxford, in Cambridgeshire, the unit entertained the Fleet Street press for the first time on 4 May 1939, when this photograph was taken. All 11 of these machines conducted a flypast of Duxford as the culmination of the Press Day.

Bf 109E. With its 500-strong workforce fully occupied producing fuselages, Supermarine had to sub-contract work on the wings out to General Aircraft and Pobjoy, wing ribs to Westland, leading edges to The Pressed Steel Company, ailerons and elevators to Aero Engines Ltd, tails to Folland, wingtips to General Electric and fuselage frames to J. Samuel White & Company. Final assembly and engine installation was completed at Eastleigh.

The Air Ministry was so dismayed by this convoluted process that in 1938 it contracted the Nuffield Organisation (which mass-produced cars) to build 1,000 Spitfire IIs in a new Shadow Factory at Castle Bromwich, and the first of these aircraft was delivered to the RAF in early July 1940. Again, these Spitfires were also delayed by various factors: changes to the production specification by the Air Ministry, the factory management's ignorance about aerospace technology and squabbles between the unions and management over pay. However, once war was declared Britain successfully converted to a war economy, with a huge drive resulting in Spitfire production eventually outstripping the German fighter production.

By then the production Spitfire I had matured into a frontline fighter to rival the best in the world. Amongst the numerous changes made to the aircraft was the replacement of the original two-bladed, fixed-pitch Watts wooden propeller with a three-bladed two-pitch or variable-pitch de Havilland or Rotol airscrew. The low, flat cockpit canopy had been replaced by a bulged canopy, thus giving more headroom for taller pilots, whilst steel armour had been fitted behind and beneath the pilot's seat. A thick slab of laminated glass was also fitted to the front of the windscreen, and Identification Friend or Foe (IFF) transponders were built into the aircraft to identify the fighter as friendly to all-new radar stations along the coast of Great Britain.

No. 19 Sqn became the first unit in Fighter Command to receive Spitfire Is in August 1938, and by September of the following year the RAF had ten squadrons equipped with the aircraft.

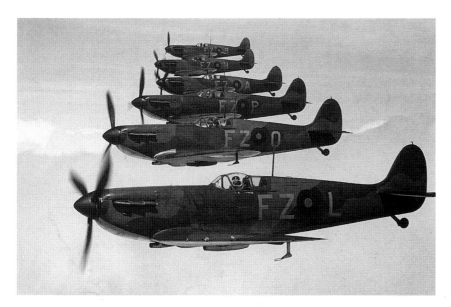

Future 27-victory ace Flg Off Robert Stanford Tuck leads a six-aircraft formation of No. 65 Sqn Spitfire Is up from RAF Hornchurch, in Essex, during a press photo-flight in the summer of 1939. The squadron had transitioned to some of the first three-bladed Spitfires to reach Fighter Command in March of that year. Tuck, who would claim 12 and two shared victories with the Spitfire I in 1940, 'made ace' with No. 65 Sqn during the Dunkirk evacuation.

It would now be just a matter of months before the world's best fighters of the period would meet in combat for the first time.

Bf 109

The Spitfire's great rival in the skies for much of World War II was the Bf 109. Design work on this aeroplane commenced in secret in March 1934 at the Bayerische Flugzeugwerke AG (BFW) facility in Augsburg-Haunstetten, in Bavaria. The company had a long history of aircraft construction, having taken over the Udet Flugzeugbau in July 1926. BFW had merged with fellow aircraft manufacturer Messerschmitt Flugzeugbau at this time, and company founder, Diplomingenieur (Dipl.-Ing. – Diploma Engineer) Willy Messerschmitt, assumed design control within the new enterprise.

German industry had been banned from producing military aircraft under the terms of the 1919 Treaty of Versailles, so manufacturers gained experience in the late 1920s and early 1930s building a series of ever more advanced mailplanes, airliners, touring and sports aircraft. Many advanced aviation design techniques such as low-set cantilever wings, stressed-skin semi-monocoque fuselage shells, retractable undercarriages and enclosed cockpits were incorporated into these machines made by manufacturers such as Heinkel, Arado, Dornier, Focke-Wulf and, of course, Messerschmitt.

Despite the restrictive Treaty of Versailles, senior officers in the Wehrmacht had secretly set up organizations in the 1920s to train future pilots for the air force. When, on 1 March 1933, Reich Chancellor Adolf Hitler announced the existence of the newly created Luftwaffe, it had sufficient pilots available to staff a number of units thanks to the various clandestine training schools run in the USSR.

The civil ministry created to oversee the running of the Luftwaffe was the Reichsluftfahrtministerium (RLM), headed by Hermann Göring. The department responsible for aviation design within the RLM was the Technische Amt (LC), and its requirements would exert considerable influence on the final configuration of the Bf 109.

As the Luftwaffe's fighter force, the Jagdwaffe (fighter arm) was initially equipped with Heinkel He 51 and Arado Ar 68 biplanes. These aircraft had braced

Bf 109E-4 OF I.(J)/LG 2

28ft 4.5in.

8ft 2.333in.

32ft 4.5in.

and staggered wings, fixed, spatted, undercarriages and open cockpits, making them little removed from the fighters of World War I. Indeed, they were slower than civilian monoplane types such as the He 70, and only marginally faster than the He 111.

Clearly something had to be done to modernize the German fighter force, and on 6 July 1933 the RLM's LCII (Technical Office for Development) issued the Tactical Requirements for Fighter Aircraft (Land) document. This stated that the Luftwaffe needed a single-seat daytime fighter armed with two fixed machine guns (with 500 rounds per gun) or one fixed cannon (100 rounds). It had to have a radio for air-to-air and air-to-ground communication, as well as a safety harness, oxygen system, parachute and heating for the pilot. The fighter had to be able to maintain a speed of 250mph for up to 20 minutes at 19,500ft, take no longer than 17 minutes to reach this height and possess at least an hour's flight duration. Its ultimate ceiling was to be 33,000ft.

From a handling perspective, the aircraft had to be capable of diving and turning without losing altitude, and easily be recoverable from a spin. The fighter also had to be operable from the average German airfield (which was 1,300ft x 1,300ft in size) by an average frontline pilot. It would also be required to fly in cloud and fog and to perform group (up to nine aircraft) take-offs and landings. Finally, the design had to be small enough to enable it to be transported by rail.

Having already built fighters for the Luftwaffe, Arado, Heinkel and Focke-Wulf were seen as front runners to win this lucrative contract, and Messerschmitt, which had no experience in designing fighters, was seen as the rank outsider. However, the latter company's series of fast sports aircraft from the late 1920s and early 1930s, boasting low-set, cantilever wings, gave LCII the confidence to instruct Messerschmitt to build a four-seater touring aircraft to compete in the 1934 European Flying Contest. The M 23 design by Willy Messerschmitt had won this prestigious international competition in 1929 and 1930, and the new aircraft produced by the company was eventually designated the Bf 108.

Many features embodied in this advanced machine would soon find their way into the Bf 109 prototype, including flush-riveted stressed-skin construction, cantilevered monoplane wings equipped with Handley Page 'slots' along the leading edges (improving the aircraft's slow-speed handling), and a narrow track undercarriage that was attached to the fuselage and retracted outwards into wells forward of the main spar.

Although it did not win the 1934 contest, the Bf 108 was the fastest machine at the meet by some margin, and it would ultimately enjoy a long career with the Luftwaffe as a utility/training aircraft.

Buoyed by this success, Messerschmitt pressed on with the Bf 109, which incorporated all of the features previously mentioned. Aside from the wing 'slots', the aircraft also had trailing-edge flaps, and these two features combined with the wing's small surface area (made possible by the growing power of aero engines) to ultimately give the Bf 109 unmatched manoeuvrability. The fuselage itself was made of light metal as a monocoque structure of roughly oval section, constructed in two halves and joined along the centre line.

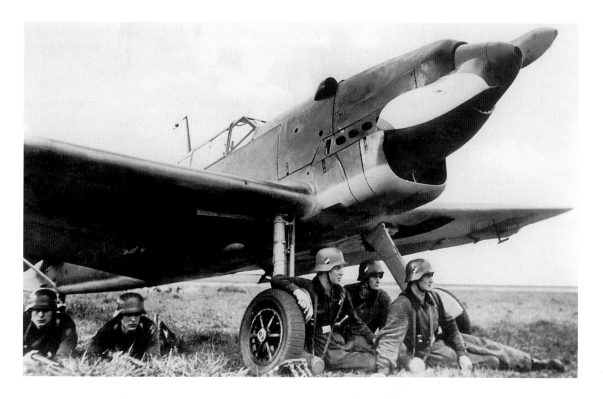

Right from the start, Messerschmitt had planned that the lightweight Bf 109 would be powered by one of the new-generation inverted-Vee 12-cylinder engines under development by Junkers and Daimler-Benz. The former's 680hp Jumo 210 was ultimately selected because it was at a more advanced stage in its development than the 960hp DB 600Aa. As it transpired, delivery of the Junkers powerplant was delayed to the point where the first prototype Bf 109 V1 had to be fitted with a 695hp Rolls-Royce Kestrel VI engine.

Construction of the V1 was completed by early May 1935, and following a series of taxiing trials, on the 28th of that month Messerschmitt's senior test pilot, Hans-Dietrich 'Bubi' Knoetzsch, made the fighter's first flight from Augsburg-Haunstetten airfield. Following initial factory trials, the aircraft was sent to the Rechlin-based *Erprobungsstelle* (testing centre) for service trials. The latter soon proved that the Bf 109 was considerably faster and more manoeuvrable than its primary rival for the fighter contract, Heinkel's He 112 V1 (which was also Kestrel-powered).

The Jumo 210A-powered Bf 109 V2 took to the skies in October 1935 and joined the trials programme three months later. This aircraft also boasted two 7.9mm MG 17 machine guns in the fuselage upper decking. The V3, which had provision for an engine-mounted 20mm MG FF/M cannon firing through the propeller hub, flew for the first time in June 1936, and a short while later both Messerschmitt and Heinkel received contracts from the RLM to build ten pre-production aircraft.

In the autumn of that year the official trials culminated in a series of tests at Travemünde, where the Bf 109 proved its superiority in a memorable flight demonstration that included tailslides, flick rolls, 21-turn spins, tight turns and terminal

This propaganda photograph shows an early Bf 109B, fitted with a provisional wooden Schwarz propeller, being used to provide cover for Wehrmacht infantrymen during maneouvres held in mid-1937. The first Messerschmitt fighters had reached the Luftwaffe in February of that year.

17

dives. Being faster in level speed and in the climb than the He 112, and easily able to outdive the Heinkel, the Bf 109 could also perform much tighter turns thanks to its leading-edge slots. From rank outsider, Messerschmitt had become the obvious choice for the fighter contract, and the Bf 109 was duly announced the competition winner.

The first of ten pre-production Bf 109B-0s took to the air in November 1936, and the following month three aircraft were sent to war-torn Spain for an evaluation under operational conditions with the Condor Legion. The trials were beset with problems, but they did give both Messerschmitt and the Luftwaffe experience of what to expect when production Bf 109Bs entered service in Germany in February 1937.

Early Bf 109Bs were built at Messerschmitt's Augsburg-Haunstetten plant, but it soon became obvious that a larger factory would be required. A new site at Regensburg was duly developed, and production of the 'Bertha' was soon transferred there. However, the company's design offices remained at Augsburg.

The first production Bf 109Bs were issued to II./JG 132 'Richthofen' at Jüterbog-Damm as replacements for the Geschwader's He 51 biplanes in February 1937. (Geschwader denotes a wing of aircraft; for more details on the structure of the Luftwaffe's fighter arm see the Unit Organization section on p. 35) However, the dominance of the Republican forces' I-15 and I-16 Ratas in Spanish skies resulted in 16 Berthas being shipped to Spain just weeks after their delivery to the Luftwaffe. Accompanying them were II./JG 132 personnel, who formed 2./J 88. Operational by April, the unit ultimately did not see its first combat until the battle for Brunete in July, when it was discovered that the Bf 109B and the nimble Soviet-built Polikarpov fighters were evenly matched below 10,000ft. At higher altitudes, the Bertha was untouchable, and German pilots soon worked out that Republican aircraft could be easily picked off if attacked from above and behind using high-speed dives – this would be the Bf 109 pilot's stock tactic throughout World War II as well.

In Germany, meanwhile, development of the aircraft continued at a rapid pace, and in June 1937 the Bf 109 V10 flew for the first time with the promising 960hp Daimler-Benz DB 600Aa fitted. This new powerplant was much longer and heavier than the Jumo, and in order to offset the shift in the aircraft's centre of gravity, Messerschmitt redesigned the fighter's cooling system. A shallow radiator bath was fitted under the nose and two radiators positioned beneath the wings. A three-bladed VDM propeller also replaced the two-blade VDM-Hamilton airscrew fitted to the Jumo-powered Bf 109B. Due to the fighter's higher all-up weight (when fully fuelled and armed), its fuselage and undercarriage were also strengthened. This aircraft would effectively serve as the prototype for the Bf 109E.

The new fighter made its entrance on the international stage in late July 1937 when three Jumo- and two Daimler-Benz-powered Bf 109s were dispatched to the 4th International Flying Meeting at Zurich-Dübendorf, in Switzerland. Setting a series of speed records during the week-long event, the aircraft garnered Messerschmitt world recognition for its Bf 109.

By year-end, production of the B model had commenced at the Gerhard Fieseler Werke at Kassel, and four *Gruppen* (groups) within the Luftwaffe and two *Staffeln* (squadrons) in Spain had re-equipped with the aircraft.

In the early spring of 1938 deliveries of the Bf 109C, fitted with the 730hp fuel-injected Jumo 210Ga engine and wing-mounted machine guns, commenced, with the first aircraft being issued to I./JG 132. Only 58 were built prior to production switching to the four-gun Bf 109D, which was powered by the 680hp carburettored Jumo 210Da engine. Some 657 were built, with aircraft also being constructed by Erla Maschinenwerk in Leipzig and Focke-Wulf Flugzeugbau of Bremen.

Aside from service with the Luftwaffe, a handful of C and D models were also sent to Spain for service with the Condor Legion, where they continued to down Nationalist Polikarpov fighters with regularity. Amongst the leading aces from this campaign were Werner Mölders (14 kills), Wolfgang Schellmann (12 kills) and Harro Harder (11 kills), all of whom would enjoy more success with the Bf 109E in the first 18 months of World War II.

While the Luftwaffe's fighter pilots continued to gain valuable combat experience in Spain, at home, the Jagdwaffe's enlargement continued apace. By 19 September 1938, a total of 583 Bf 109B/C/Ds were on strength, but limited availability of the Daimler-Benz engine had stymied plans for the rapid fielding of the Bf 109E. This was

A team of armourers load ammunition boxes for the engine- mounted MG 17 machine guns fitted to an early-build Bf 109E-1. Each gun had sufficient ammunition storage for 1,000 rounds. Note that the groundcrew have removed an area of the cowling immediately forward of the cockpit so as to gain easy access to the guns and ammunition boxes.

because bomber production had priority over fighter procurement in the late 1930s, and most of the DB 600s produced were duly allocated to the He 111. Finally, in 1938 the focus shifted to fighter production, and by then the much delayed DB 601A was at last reaching maturity, so Daimler-Benz switched its efforts to perfecting this powerplant. This new engine was very similar to the DB 600, but crucially it featured fuel injection rather than a float carburettor. The engine meant that the Bf 109 could perform negative G flight, and also increased the fighter's range through improved fuel economy.

With its DB 601A engine rated at 1,175hp for take-off, the Bf 109E-1, nicknamed the 'Emil', finally entered series production in December 1938, the new aircraft boasting unmatched take-off and climb performance. The higher wing loading of the Emil increased the fighter's turning circle and stall speed, but it was still very much a pilot's aircraft. Like the D model before it, the E-1's armament consisted of two MG 17s in the upper fuselage decking and two more machine guns in the wings. The latter had 500 rounds per gun, and the fuselage guns had 1,000 rounds each. The aircraft was fitted with a Revi C/12C gunsight and FuG 7 radio, the latter having a range of about 40 miles.

In early 1939 the first Bf 109E-3s began rolling off the production line, these aircraft having their wing MG 17s replaced with MG FF 20mm cannon as initially trialled in the Bf 109C-3. Each weapon only had 60 rounds, but their destructive punch was unrivalled. Once in frontline service, the E-3 *Kanonenmaschine* (cannon machine) was rated as the best early generation Messerschmitt by those that flew it, with the aircraft enjoying a greater margin of superiority over its rivals than any other Bf 109 variant.

Some 40 Bf 109E-1/3s were sent to Spain for service with the Condor Legion, although it appears that these aircraft did not get the chance to prove themselves in aerial combat prior to the Republicans surrendering in March 1939.

A total of 200 German pilots had flown with Jagdgruppe (Fighter Group) 88 in Spain, and these men would be in the vanguard of the Jagdwaffe's fighting force during the first 18 months of World War II. They would primarily be flying Bf 109Es during this period, and between 1 January and 1 September 1939, 1,091 Emils were delivered. Four engine plants had been established to allow production of the DB 601 to keep up pace with airframe construction, with Bf 109s being built by Messerschmitt at Regensburg, and by Erla and Fieseler, as well as by the Wiener-Neüstadt Flugzeugbau in Austria.

By the time the Wehrmacht advanced east into Poland on 1 September 1939, no fewer than 28 Gruppen were operating Bf 109B/C/D/Es. The Messerschmitt fighter was now well placed to dominate the skies over Europe.

TECHNICAL SPECIFICATIONS

SPITFIRE

PROTOTYPE SPITFIRE K5054

Remarkably, just one prototype Spitfire was built by Vickers Supermarine in the form of K5054. This aircraft conducted all the pre-production development work associated with the aircraft between 5 March 1936 and the first flight of the premier production Spitfire I (K9787) on 14 May 1938. Thoroughly tested by both the manufacturer and the RAF, the hand-built K5054 was progressively altered during this period to more closely represent the 310 Spitfire Is ordered by the Air Ministry in mid-1936. Guns were installed and fired in flight, a modified propeller fitted to improve its top speed and the external skin finishing changed to help reduce the time and cost involved in building production Spitfires. Improved versions of the Rolls-Royce engine were also progressively installed, including the Merlin 'C' (later designated the Merlin II) of 990hp, the Merlin 'F' of 1,035hp and finally the Merlin III of 1,030hp. Gun heating trials were also undertaken with this aircraft. Badly damaged twice in its brief lifetime during landing accidents, K5054 soldiered on in its testing role until late October 1938, by which time some of the 20 production Spitfire Is that had flown by then were conducting trials work. Sent to Farnborough to serve as a 'high-speed' hack, the aircraft was finally written off on 4 September 1939 in a fatal landing accident.

SPITFIRE I

The jig-built Spitfire I differed significantly from the hand-built K5054 in a number of key areas, primarily internally. The fighter's distinctive elliptical wing had been considerably strengthened so as to raise its never-to-be-exceeded maximum speed from 380mph to 470mph. Flap travel was also increased from 57° to 90°, and fuel tankage boosted from 75 to 84 gal. Other equipment and minor changes were also introduced, which resulted in the first production Spitfire I weighing in at 5,819lb fully loaded – 460lb heavier than K5054. The first 64 airframes were fitted with the Merlin II engine, whilst the remaining Spitfire I/IAs were powered by the 1,030hp Merlin III. From the 78th airframe onwards, the Rolls-Royce engine would be driving a three-bladed de Havilland or Rotol two-pitch or constant speed propeller, rather than the Watts two-bladed fixed-pitch wooden airscrew. The new propeller shortened the take-off run from 420 yards to 225 yards (with the constant-speed airscrew), increased the rate of climb, boosted the top speed from 361mph to 365mph and made the Spitfire much easier to handle in combat. The first Spitfire Is reached No. 19 Sqn in August 1938, and further modifications were brought in following early months of service flying. Engine start problems were cured with a more powerful starter motor, an engine-driven hydraulic system to raise and lower the undercarriage replaced the hand pump that was originally fitted, and a bulged canopy was introduced to provide the extra headroom that was needed to allow taller pilots to fly the aircraft in comfort. Early in World War II, once it became clear that pilots of modern fighters needed armour protection, the previously unarmoured Spitfire I had a thick slab of laminated glass fitted to the front of its windscreen. A 0.12in.-thick light alloy cover was also fitted over the upper fuel tank in the fuselage, and 75lb of steel armour was installed

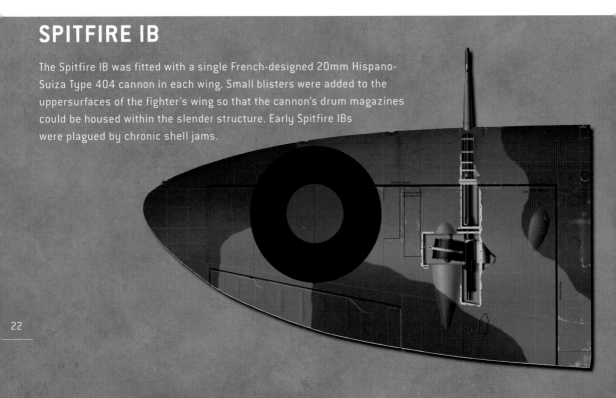

SPITFIRE IB

The Spitfire IB was fitted with a single French-designed 20mm Hispano-Suiza Type 404 cannon in each wing. Small blisters were added to the uppersurfaces of the fighter's wing so that the cannon's drum magazines could be housed within the slender structure. Early Spitfire IBs were plagued by chronic shell jams.

behind and beneath the pilot's seat. In the spring of 1940, the RAF also introduced 100 octane fuel in place of the 87 octane that it had previously used. The Spitfire I's Merlin engine had to be modified to use this petrol, and the higher octane allowed pilots to select double the supercharger boost for a maximum of five minutes (raising the top speed by up to 34mph) without the risk of damaging the Merlin III. IFF transponder equipment was also introduced soon after the outbreak of war, thus allowing radar operators on the ground to identify the aircraft they were tracking on their plots. Finally, just prior to the Battle of Britain commencing, all frontline Spitfires were fitted with 'two-step' rudder pedals, with the upper step six inches higher than the lower step. Just prior to combat, the pilot lifted his feet on to the upper steps, thus giving his body a more horizontal posture, which in turn raised his blackout threshold by about 1 G, allowing him to sustain tighter turns in action. Production of the Spitfire I ran from April 1938 through to March 1941, by which time 1,567 examples had been built.

SPITFIRE IA

In the summer of 1940, non-Castle-Bromwich-built aircraft that were still equipped with eight Browning 0.303-in. machine guns were redesignated Spitfire IAs so as to differentiate them from the recently introduced cannon-armed Spitfire IBs.

SPITFIRE IB

Soon after the Spitfire I entered service, the RAF stated that it required the fighter to pack a heavier punch in order to down bombers that boasted armour and

SPITFIRE I/II

The Spitfire I/II boasted four Browning 0.303-in. machine guns in each wing. Although the Brownings were very reliable, they were regularly criticised by RAF pilots for not providing them with sufficient punch when it came to shooting down German fighters and bombers.

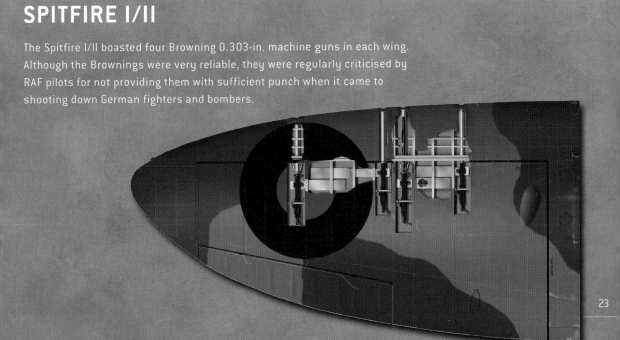

self-sealing tanks. Having evaluated a series of heavier-calibre cannon, it selected the French 20mm Hispano-Suiza Type 404 as the best weapon of its size then in production. The cannon boasted a high muzzle velocity and the ability to fire armour-piercing shells, and a deal was quickly struck with the manufacturer to build the gun under licence in the UK. In June 1939, Spitfire I L1007 was fitted with two cannon in place of all eight machine guns, and the following month it commenced flight testing at Martlesham Heath. Small blisters were added to the upper surfaces of the fighter's wing so that the cannon's drum magazines could be housed within the slender structure. The cannon barrels also extended from the leading edges of the wings. The Hispano-Suiza guns had to be mounted in the thin wings on their sides in order for them to fit, and if they were fired when the fighter was pulling G, used cartridge cases tended to bounce back into the cannon and cause stoppages. If only one gun jammed, the recoil forces from the remaining weapon made it virtually impossible for the pilot to accurately sight his target. RAF engineers worked hard to solve these problems, and by the spring of 1940 the armament was deemed reliable enough to enter series production. The first examples were delivered to No. 19 Sqn at Duxford in June 1940, but when the unit went into action two months later its aircraft were plagued with chronic cannon jams, and the Spitfire IBs were hastily replaced with all-machine gun Spitfire IIAs within days. During the autumn further work was done to rectify the jamming problem, and to address the issue of the weapon's modest 60-round magazine per cannon – enough ammunition for just five seconds' worth of firing – it was decided to retain four 0.303-in. Brownings in the outer troughs, and the first of these revised Spitfire IBs was issued to No. 92 Sqn in November 1940.

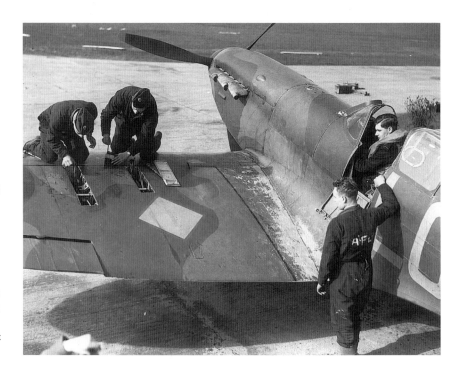

The Spitfire I's eight guns, and associated ammunition bays, were covered by 22 panels secured by 150 half-turn Dzus fastners. It was estimated that a proficient four-man re-arming team could turn a Spitfire around in 30 minutes. This No. 602 'City of Glasgow' Sqn aircraft was photographed at Drem, in East Lothian, in April 1940.

SPITFIRE IIA/B

Following a series of delays, the massive Shadow Factory established by the Nuffield Organisation in Castle Bromwich at last began to produce Spitfires in June 1940. These aircraft were virtually identical to late-production Spitfire Is built elsewhere in the UK, but they were fitted with the slightly more powerful Merlin XII engine that produced 110hp more than the Merlin III. Designated the Spitfire IIA, the first examples were delivered to No. 611 Sqn in July 1940, followed by Nos 19, 74 and 266 Sqns. Towards the end of the aircraft's production run at Nuffield, 170 cannon-armed Spitfire IIBs were built at the factory, these aircraft also boasting four 0.303-in. machine guns. By the time production of the Spitfire IIA ended in July 1941, 751 examples had been built.

SPITFIRE IIA LONG RANGE

Operations over Dunkirk in May–June 1940 had revealed the Spitfire's limited radius of action, so Supermarine looked to extend its fighter's range through the provision of an external tank. Spitfire I P9565 flew with a 30-gal tank fitted beneath its port wing in the summer of 1940, but the advent of the Battle of Britain stymied development until Fighter Command commenced offensive operations into Europe in early 1941. Eventually, 60 Spitfire IIA Long Range (LR) fighters were built with a 40-gal fixed tank fitted under the port wing, these lop-sided aircraft initially seeing service in the spring of 1941. Although less manoeuvrable and 26mph slower than a standard Spitfire IIA, the tank-equipped fighter carried nearly half as much fuel again, thus making it ideally suited to bomber escort missions.

This Spitfire II (LR) was one of 60 aircraft built with a 40-gal fixed tank fitted under the port wing and used by Fighter Command for long-range bomber escort missions from the spring of 1941 through to year-end. Because of their paucity in numbers, these aircraft were routinely swapped between units operating in Nos 10 and 11 Groups. This particular Spitfire II (LR) is marked up with No. 66 Sqn's 'LZ' codes.

Bf 109

The Bf 109E was the dominant model of the Messerschmitt to serve during the Battle of Britain. All major derivatives of this model are described in detail below.

Bf 109 V10

This pre-production Bf 109 started life fitted with a 730hp Junkers Jumo 210Ga direct fuel-injection engine. In June 1937 this powerplant was replaced by a 960hp Daimler-Benz DB 600Aa. The Bf 109 V11, V12, V13 and V14 (the latter two participating in the 4th International Flying Meeting in Switzerland, in July 1937) were also subsequently flown with the DB 600Aa. All four aircraft featured a redesigned engine cooling system that saw a shallow oil radiator bath replace the huge coolant radiator beneath the nose of the Jumo-powered Bf 109, and rectangular coolant radiators under each wing replace the small oil radiator beneath the port wing. The upper cowling was also revised, with the supercharger air intake on the upper starboard side being replaced by an intake midway down the port side. Finally, a three-bladed VDM propeller was fitted in place of the two-blade VDM-Hamilton airscrew employed by the Jumo-powered Bf 109B. This trio of aircraft served as the prototypes for the Bf 109E which would follow in late 1938.

Bf 109 V14-16

These three V-series aircraft were fitted with the early-development DB 601A engines of 1,050hp in the summer of 1938, although the reliability of the powerplant was so poor that the introduction of the Bf 109E-1 to frontline service was delayed until year-end. Previously powered by a DB 600Aa, the V14 was fitted with two MG FF 20mm cannon in the wings and a pair of MG 17 7.92mm machine guns in the fuselage. The V15 had only the latter weapons installed.

Bf 109E-0

A pre-production series of ten Bf 109E-0s was built for service evaluation and engine and armament development in the autumn of 1938. These aircraft were very similar to the V14, but they were all armed with two fuselage- and two wing-mounted MG 17s.

Bf 109E-1

With final clearance of the DB 601A for service use in late 1938, production of the Bf 109E-1 had commenced in earnest by year-end. Indeed, a substantial number of engineless airframes had been stored from the autumn of 1938 at Augsburg-Haunstetten pending the availability of powerplants. The E-1 was exclusively equipped with MG 17s, two in the fuselage and one in each wing. Some 1,540 E-1s were built at four manufacturing plants in Germany and Austria in 1939 alone. In 1940, a number of E-1s were factory-modified into E-1/B fighter-bombers with the fitment of ETC 500/IXb or ETC 50/VIIId bomb racks on the fuselage centre line. A number of E-1/Ns were also built following the replacement of the standard DB 601A engine with the 1,270hp DB 601N that had flattened instead of concave piston heads for improved compression, and used 96 octane C3 fuel. The E-1/B Jagdbomber concept was tested in combat by Erprobungsgruppe (Operational Test Group) 210 during anti-shipping operations in the Channel in July 1940. Used principally as a dive-bomber, dropping bombs ranging in size from 110 to 551lb, the aircraft enjoyed great success. Indeed, every Jagdgeschwader was ordered to create a Jabo Staffel during the summer of 1940, and numerous E-1s, E-3s and E-4s were modified into Jagdbombers.

This rare colour photograph shows two Bf 109E-3s from III./JG 2 at Querqueville, in Normandy, in late August 1940. The aircraft in the foreground is believed to have belonged to Oberleutnant Werner Machold, who would be credited with the destruction of 13 Spitfires in 1940–41.

Bf 109E-3

In the early summer of 1939 a pre-production E-0 had been equipped with the improved 1,175hp DB 601Aa engine intended for the E-3 and flown as the Bf 109 V17. This version of the Daimler-Benz engine could mount an MG FF 20mm cannon on its crankcase, the weapon in turn firing through the airscrew hub. However, the problems of vibration, seizing and overheating that had beset the engine-mounted MG FF in the Bf 109D-1 persisted, and the weapon was rarely used in frontline service. The two wing-mounted MG FFs that replaced the MG 17s in the E-3 were retained, with each weapon being fed by a 60-round magazine. Production E-3s began to replace the E-1 on the assembly lines in late 1939 – the armament was the only thing that differentiated an E-1 from an E-3, and the latter proved to be the most-produced E-series fighter. E-3s were also retrofitted with a series of revisions following lessons learned during the French campaign in May–June 1940, including 8mm armour for the pilot, seat armour and a curved armour plate over the pilot's head that was attached to the hinged canopy. Heavier framing and flatter, squarer Plexiglas panels in the folding part of the canopy hood also began to appear in the early summer of 1940, these being more economical to produce than the original transparencies. Like the E-1, E-3/B and E-3/N variants were constructed in 1940, and many more were rebuilt as E-4s and E-7s.

Bf 109E-4

Nearly identical to the E-3, the E-4, which entered production in mid-1940, had the engine-mounted MG FF finally discarded. The aircraft featured two new MG FF/M

Oberstleutnant Adolf Galland, Kommodore of JG 26, taxies his Bf109E-4/N on the gravel strip at Abbeville on 23 December 1940.

Ready for action, this Bf 109E-4/B of I.(J)/LG 2 was photographed at Marquise in October 1940. It has been loaded with four SC 50 bombs on a centerline rack, each of the weapons being fitted with whistles on the fins to enhance their noise when falling. The fighter-bomber bears the 2. *Staffel* top hat emblem on its rear fuselage.

cannon in the wings, these weapons boasting an improved rate of fire over the 20mm cannon installed in the E-3. Armour plating was fitted to protect the fuselage fuel tank and head armour was installed in the canopy. Many E-4s were not new production aircraft, instead being factory-modified E-1s and E-3s. Again, E-4/B and E-4/N variants were produced too. In early 1941 Bf 109E-4s of I./JG 27 that were destined for operations in the Mediterranean and North Africa were tropicalized through the fitment of a dust filter over the supercharger air intake and the installation of a emergency desert survival equipment. These aircraft were redesignated E-4/N Trops.

Bf 109E-5/6

Built in small numbers alongside the E-4, the E-5 variant had its wing cannon removed and a single vertical Zeiss Rb 21/18 camera mounted in the rear fuselage immediately behind the cockpit. The E-6 retained its full armament, but featured a smaller Rb 12.5/7 x 9 camera, again aft of the cockpit. A small number of tropicalized E-5/Trops were also operated by I./JG 27 in early 1941.

Bf 109E-7

Evolved directly from the E-4/N, the E-7 differed primarily in its ability to carry either a 66-gal auxiliary drop tank or bombs of differing weights (E-7/B). The E model's relatively modest range had proven an embarrassment for the Jagdstaffeln during the final phases of the invasion of France, and a rack and jettisonable drop tank made of moulded plywood were duly produced. The tank leaked badly, and pilots suspected that it would easily ignite in combat, so it saw no operational service through to the end of 1940. Factory-installed internal drop tank connections, a bomb-release mechanism and associated wiring were fitted into the E-7 as standard equipment, and this allowed units in the field quickly to convert fighter-bomber-configured aircraft into extended-range fighters, and vice-versa – the E-7 and near-identical E-8 were the

Bf 109E-4 COWLING GUNS

Like previous versions of the Emil, the Bf 109E-4 was fitted with a pair of
Rheinmetall MG 17s immediately above its DB 601 engine. Each weapon had a
magazine holding 1,000 rounds per gun. Note how the guns are staggered, with
the port MG 17 being set slightly forward the width of the ammunition feed chute.

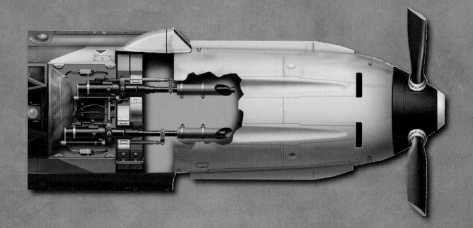

Bf 109E-4 WING GUN

The Oerlikon MG FF 'M' 20mm cannon made its frontline debut in the Bf 109E-4.
This version of the weapon fired M-Geschosse (Mine) shells, which inflicted more
damage than a standard round. Boasting a low cyclic rate of fire, pronounced recoil
and oversized Trommel T60 drum magazine, the weapon was replaced by the superb
MG 151 from late 1940.

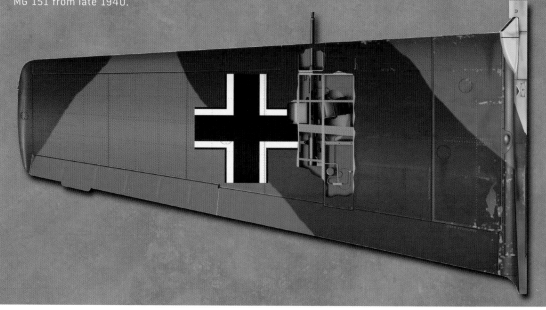

only E-model aircraft capable of carrying the drop tank. Operational experience with the E-1/B, E-3/B and E-4/B had shown that the aircraft's engine was forced to work harder to overcome the drag associated with external stores, so Messerschmitt fitted an extra 2-gal oil tank to help improve lubrication of the DB 601 when operating at higher power settings. The first E-7s reached frontline units in France in August 1940, and again many of these aircraft were not new production machines, but factory-modified E-1s, E-3s and E-4s. A Bf 109E-7 Trop variant was also produced in 1941, and later that same year the Bf 109E-7/Z introduced a nitrous oxide power boosting system (GM 1) to the DB 601N, thus turning those aircraft fitted with this equipment into high-altitude fighters.

Bf 109E-8 AND -9

The E-8 and -9 were the final versions of the E series produced by Messerschmitt. All were rebuilt E-1s, E-3s and E-4s, and appeared in the autumn of 1940. The principal innovation of these aircraft was the introduction of the DB 601E, which was capable of generating 1,350hp thanks to increased revolutions and improved supercharging. Additional back armour was also added, and as with the E-7, the E-8 could carry a drop tank. The E-8/N was fitted with the DB 601N engine rather than the E-series powerplant, and the E-8/B boasted bomb-rack modifications. A Bf 109E-8 Trop variant was also produced in 1941. Finally, the Bf 109E-9 was the reconnaissance version of the E-8, with an Rb 50/30 camera located in the rear fuselage. The last E-series Bf 109 was finally completed in early 1942, by which time more than 4,000 had been built.

Bf 109E-3 AND SPITFIRE IA COMPARISON SPECIFICATIONS		
	Bf 109E-3	**Spitfire IA**
Powerplant	1,175hp DB 601Aa	1,030hp Merlin III
Dimensions		
Span	32ft 4.5in.	36ft 10in.
Length	28ft 4.5in.	29ft 11in.
Height	8ft 2.333in.	12ft 7.75in.
Wing area	174.05 sq ft	242 sq ft
Weights		
Empty	4,685lb	4,517lb
Loaded	5,875lb	5,844lb
Performance		
Max speed	348mph at 15,000ft	346mph at 15,000ft
Range	410 miles	415 miles
Climb	to 20,000ft in 7.75 min	to 20,000ft in 7.42 min
Service ceiling	34,450ft	30,500ft
Armament	2 x 20mm MG FF 2 x 7.92mm MG 17	8 x 0.303-in. Brownings

THE STRATEGIC SITUATION

The vulnerability of southern England to aerial attacks had been graphically shown during the Zeppelin and Gotha bomber offensives of World War I. British biplane scouts had struggled to defend London and other cities in the region, and following the fall of France to the German forces in June 1940, south-east England steeled itself once again for an assault from the skies. In the vanguard of this defence would be 19 Spitfire squadrons assigned to RAF Fighter Command. Their principal opponent in the skies during 1940 would be the much-vaunted, and combat-proven, Bf 109E, which had initially seen action in the Luftwaffe's highly successful aerial campaign that had been waged as part of the revolutionary *Blitzkrieg* (lit. 'lightning war') offensive, firstly in Poland and then in western Europe. Blitzkrieg had seen the Wehrmacht's mechanized infantry, supported by Panzers and waves of fighters and bombers, capture huge swathes of territory in just a matter of days.

Yet despite the German success in Poland, the Bf 109 had played only a peripheral part in the 18-day air war. This was primarily because it was feared that French and British bombers would attack German cities upon their countries' declaration of war in support of Poland on 3 September. Those units that were involved duly found aerial targets elusive to come by, and most of the 67 Bf 109s lost during the campaign fell victim to ground fire as pilots searched for well-hidden Polish aircraft.

In between the invasion of Poland and the launching of the Blitzkrieg in the west on 10 May 1940, Bf 109 units, like the rest of the Luftwaffe, endured the *Sitzkrieg* (lit. 'sitting down war'), or the 'Phoney War', as it was dubbed by the Allies. Aircraft from both sides would periodically venture across their respective defensive borders (the Maginot line in France and the Westwall or Siegfried line in Germany) on tentative reconnaissance flights. Most action during this period took place over the *Dreiländereck* (three nations corner) on the northernmost corner of the Franco-German border, as this was the shortest route for Allied reconnaissance aircraft heading for the Ruhr.

Many of the leading Bf 109E aces claimed their first victories during this period, including Oberleutnant Werner Mölders, Oberleutnant Rolf Pingel and Oberleutnant Hans von Hahn. Aside from engaging French fighters, the *Jagdflieger* (fighter pilots) also took on RAF Hurricanes that were based in France in support of the British Expeditionary Force (BEF), as well as Blenheim and Wellington bombers sent to attack German ports along the North Sea coast. The only Spitfires encountered were unarmed Photographic Development Unit (PDU) aircraft, two of which were brought down in March and April 1940. By the time the 'Phoney War' ended, the Jagdgruppen had claimed no fewer than 160 victories, and numerous Bf 109 pilots had received their first taste of aerial combat.

In a forerunner of what was to come in the Battle of Britain, practically the whole of the Lufwaffe's single-engined fighter strength was brought together for the invasion of France and the Low Countries. In all, 27 Jagdgruppen were brought forward to airfields scattered along the Westwall, these units being split between Luftflotten (Air Fleets) 2 and 3. More than 1,016 Bf 109Es and over 1,000 pilots prepared themselves to wrest control of the skies over western Europe.

The German campaign itself was divided into two parts, code-named *Gelb* (Yellow) and *Rot* (Red). Operation *Gelb* would commence with an all-out attack on Holland and Belgium, which, it was calculated, would cause the BEF and French northern armies to rush to the aid of the Low Countries. With the Allies out of their prepared

Ranking German ace of the Spanish Civil War, Werner Mölders was undoubtedly the most influential tactician in the fledgling Jagdwaffe. Seen here climbing out of his Bf 109E-3 in late August 1940, he enjoyed great success as Geschwaderkommodore of JG 51, claiming 13 Spitfires destroyed during the Battle of Britain. The first pilot to achieve 100 aerial victories, Mölders would lose his life in a flying accident on 22 November 1941, by which point his tally stood at 115 kills.

33

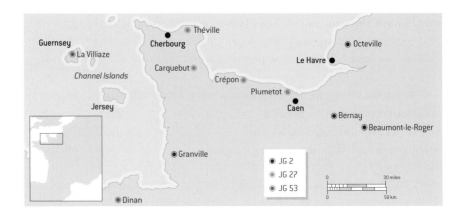

Luftwaffe single-seat fighter disposition in Normandy, Brittany and the Channel Islands during the Battle of Britain.

defensive positions along the Maginot line, the Wehrmacht would launch its primary offensive against the vulnerable rear of the Allied forces, with Panzers sweeping around behind them and racing for the Channel. The Low Countries and Anglo-French divisions would be cut off from supplies and reinforcements in the process, and thus quickly defeated. Operation *Rot* would then swing into action, with German troops advancing west across the Somme into central France.

The Jagdgruppen assigned to Luftflotte 2 would be in the vanguard of Operation *Gelb*, and the pilots of JG 2, JG 26, JG 27 and JG 51 cut swathes through the obsolescent Allied fighters that attempted to blunt the German onslaught. On 12 May, with the launching of the armoured thrust at the rear of the stretched Allied forces, Luftflotte 3's units at last joined in the action too. Two days later, during a series of actions over Sedan that saw Allied bombers attempt to destroy the strategically crucial River Meuse bridge crossings, Bf 109 units downed no fewer than 89 aircraft in an action that effectively sealed the German victory in France. Yet despite successes such as this, the campaign in the West was very much a calculated risk for the Jagdwaffe, as it possessed insufficient reserves of fighters, fuel and ammunition in order to support a sustained campaign. Fortunately, the rapidity with which Allied forces capitulated in the face of the Blitzkrieg meant that resources never reached breaking point. Indeed, just 147 Bf 109s were lost in May (including aircraft destroyed in the Norwegian campaign), followed by 88 in June.

As supply lines became stretched as the fighting in northern France reached Dunkirk, however, with serviceability amongst the Jagdgruppen reaching an all-time low due to a lack of fuel, poor parts supply, austere operating bases (often little more than farmers' fields) and sheer pilot exhaustion. Ironically, it was at this point that Bf 109 units began at last to encounter Spitfire squadrons flying from bases in southern England in support of the sea evacuation of troops from Dunkirk. RAF Fighter Command succeeded in preventing German bombers from sinking many of the vessels that transported troops back to England primarily because the Jagdstaffeln, lacking serviceable aircraft and suitable bases, could not adequately protect the vulnerable *Kampfgeschwader* (bomber wings) and *Stukageschwader* (Stuka wings) – a portent of things to come later that summer.

Although the evacuation of Dunkirk had ended on the morning of 3 June, fighting in France continued as part of Operation *Rot* until a ceasefire was agreed some 22 days later. By then, most of the Bf 109 units that had played such a key part in the success in the West had returned to Germany to rest, recuperate and refit in preparation for an all-out attack on the United Kingdom.

UNIT ORGANIZATION

As with the Blitzkrieg in the West, Luftflottenkommando 2 and 3 would again be at forefront of the fighting during the Battle of Britain, controlling all Bf 109 units assigned to the offensive through the offices of *Jagdfliegerführer* (Fighter Aircraft Command) 2 and 3.

Unlike British fighter squadrons at the time, which only officially formed into wings as the RAF went on the offensive in 1941, German fighter units had been grouped together pre-war. The Jagdwaffe equivalent of a typical 12-aircraft squadron in Fighter Command in 1940 was the Staffel, which consisted of nine aircraft (rising to as many as 16 as the war progressed). It was led by a Staffelkapitän of Oberleutnant or Hauptmann rank, who controlled a further ten pilots and around 80 groundcrew. Staffeln were usually numbered 1, 2, 3 etc.

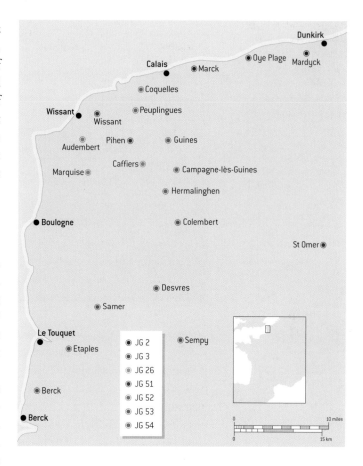

Luftwaffe single-seat fighter disposition in the Pas de Calais during the Battle of Britain.

In 1940, typically, three Staffeln and *Stab* (headquarters flight) would be assigned to a single Gruppe, which was the Luftwaffe's basic flying unit for operational and administrative purposes. Normally, one complete Gruppe occupied a single airfield, and this was typically the case during the Battle of Britain, with linked Staffeln being spread amongst austere sites in the Pas de Calais, Normandy, Brittany and the Channel Islands. The Gruppenkommandeur was usually a Hauptmann or Major, and he led somewhere between 35 and 40 pilots and more than 300 groundcrew. Gruppen were usually numbered I., II., III. etc.

The Geschwader was the largest Luftwaffe flying unit to have a fixed strength of aircraft. Eight Jagdgeschwader flew Bf 109Es during the Battle of Britain, with five (JGs 3, 26, 51, 52 and 54) assigned to Luftflottenkommando 2 in the Pas de Calais and three to Luflottenkommando 3 (JGs 2, 27 and 53) in Normandy, Brittany and the Channel Islands. Additionally, Bf 109E fighter-bombers were flown by Erprobungsgruppe 210's 1 Staffel and II.(Schl.)/LG 2. Assigned some 90–95 aircraft, the Geschwader was usually led by a Kommodore of Major, Oberleutnant or Oberst rank.

Major Werner Mölders' great friend, and rival during 1940–41 was Major Adolf Galland, Gruppenkommandeur of III./JG 26 (and later Geschwaderkommodore). This was Galland's Bf 109E-3 during the early stages of the Battle of Britain, the aircraft bearing 22 *Abschuss* (victory) bars on its rudder when this photograph was taken at Marquise.

The Jagdgeschwader were in turn locally controlled by Jagdfliegerführer (those involved in the Battle of Britain were numbered 2 and 3), which issued operational directives to the frontline flying units. The Jagdfliegerführer were in turn part of the larger, locally based *Fliegerkorps* (air corps), which were ultimately subordinated to the Luftflotten (of which the Luftwaffe had four in 1940). These were self-contained organizations, each with its own fighter, bomber, reconnaissance, ground-attack and transport units.

The Jagdwaffe slowly began to return to the Channel coast in strength during July and early August 1940, some 809 Bf 109Es being in France by 20 July, and this number increased to 934 by 10 August.

Opposing the growing ranks of German fighters were 29 squadrons of Hurricanes (462 aircraft) and 19 squadrons of Spitfires (292 aircraft). As previously mentioned, these aircraft were not organized into air fleets or groups as per the Luftwaffe model. Instead, all RAF fighters in the UK were centrally controlled by Fighter Command, headed by Air Chief Marshal Sir Hugh Dowding. The latter had calculated pre-war that he needed a minimum of 46 squadrons (typically numbering 12 aircraft) and 736 fighters to defend all possible targets in the UK ranging from Portsmouth to the River Clyde. During the Battle of France and the evacuation of Dunkirk, Fighter Command had lost around 300 aircraft, but these had been replaced by July. Therefore, Dowding felt reasonably confident that he had sufficient resources to hand to defend the UK from attacks by the Luftwaffe.

Fighter Command had been formed in 1936 as one of four commands into which the flying strength of the RAF was broken up by the Air Ministry primarily in response to the growing rearmament of Germany. With its HQ at Bentley Priory, Fighter Command initially controlled three groups created by Dowding to defend the UK. No. 11 Group was charged with protecting the south-east, No. 12 Group the Midlands and No. 13 Group the North and Scotland. On 8 July 1940, following the fall of France, 10 Group was established to cover potential targets in the south-west.

Each Group was split up into Sectors, which were given letters for identification purposes, although they were ultimately known by the name of their Sector Station, which was the airfield controlling them. Defending London and the south-east, No. 11 Group would be the vital organization in the UK's defence in 1940. Its HQ was in Uxbridge, not far from Bentley Priory, and its Sectors (centred on London) were lettered A, B, C, D, E, F and Z, controlled from Tangmere, Kenley, Biggin Hill, Hornchurch, North Weald, Debden and Northolt respectively.

The fighters based at these stations, and nearby smaller 'satellite' airfields, were the 'teeth' of Fighter Command in 1940, but the pilots flying these aircraft relied on other assets within the command to take the fight effectively to the Luftwaffe. Undoubtedly the most important of these were the chain of radar stations built during the late 1930s along the south and east coasts of England and Scotland. Code-named Chain Home (CH), the stations (there were 18 between Portsmouth and Aberdeen) were able to detect and track enemy aircraft approaching from medium or high level at distances of more than 100 miles. This equipment proved unable to track aircraft flying at altitudes below 5,000ft, however, so in late 1939 the RAF introduced Chain Home Low (CHL) stations that could detect aircraft flying at 2,000ft some 35 miles from the UK coastline. CHL sites were interspersed between the CH towers.

A complex network of landlines linking these various sites with Fighter Command HQ and Group and Sector operations rooms was another asset that proved vital during the Battle of Britain. When enemy aircraft were detected by radar, their grid position, altitude and estimated strength were passed via a landline to the Filter Centre at Fighter Command HQ. Once the plot had been classified as 'hostile', it was passed

WAAFs at the No. 11 Group operations room at Uxbridge, moving unit symbols into place to update the air picture on the situation-map table.

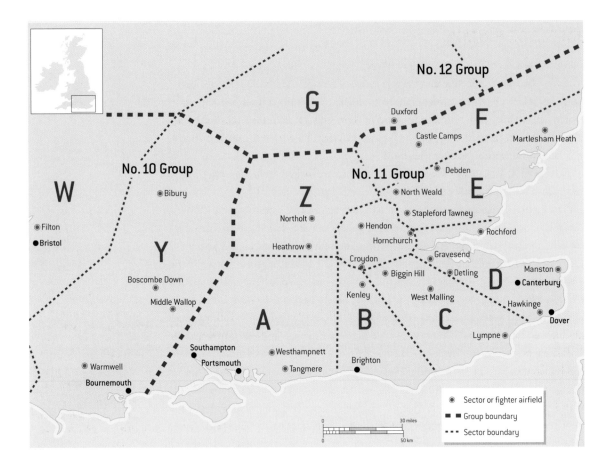

RAF Fighter Command Sector and fighter airfields in south-east England during the Battle of Britain.

to the Operations Room and noted as a marker on the situation map. This information was also relayed to relevant fighter Groups and Sector operations rooms, where it also appeared on their situation maps. The fighter controller at the Group HQ tasked with defending the area that appeared to be threatened by the 'hostile' plot then ordered his units to 'scramble'. It was crucial that this order was given early enough to allow the fighters to get up to the raiders' altitude.

Radar of this period could not track aircraft overland, so once German aircraft crossed the English coastline, the Observer Corps took over the responsibility of tracking formations. They would pass plot information via a landline to their own Group HQ, which in turn relayed details to the Fighter Command Filter Centre for onward transmission. Once airborne, a fighter unit remained under the radio control of one of the Sector operations rooms, the fighter controller guiding the squadron until it visually sighted the enemy. At this point the formation leader would call 'Tally Ho!' over the radio, signalling to the controller that he needed no further help from him.

Fighter Command squadrons were thoroughly familiar with ground-based fighter control come the summer of 1940, having regularly exercised with this system pre-war. According to noted Battle of Britain historian Dr Alfred Price, 'in the forthcoming air actions over Britain, the ground control system would be Fighter Command's Ace of trumps' (Osprey Elite 104 *Britain's Air Defences 1939–45* p. 6).

BATTLE OF BRITAIN

For the second and last time in the Luftwaffe's history, the Battle of Britain would see virtually the entire frontline strength of Bf 109Es concentrated in one area – the Channel coast. Once again, these aircraft would be charged with achieving aerial supremacy as the German Kampfgeschwader and Stukageschwader strived to knock out Fighter Command in preparation for the seaborne invasion of southern England, codenamed Operation *Sealöwe* (Sea Lion).

The Battle of Britain has been split into four phases by historians, commencing in early July with *Kanalkampf* (Channel Battle). During this period, German aircraft probed British defences primarily through attacks on coastal convoys, as well as port facilities on the south coast. Only JG 26 and JG 53 were initially assigned to this phase of the campaign, as most other Jagdgeschwader were still making good their losses suffered during the occupation of France. *Kanalkampf* would last until 12 August, and although Fighter Command succeeded in matching the Luftwaffe in trying circumstances, it had suffered significant losses – including 27 Spitfires destroyed and 51 damaged. Many of these had been claimed by Bf 109E pilots conducting *Freie Jagd* (Free Chase) sweeps independently of the bombers, seeking out RAF fighters.

The date 13 August was dubbed *Adlertag* (Eagle Day) by the Luftwaffe, and it signalled the start of the sustained campaign against RAF airfields, radar stations and other key military targets such as aircraft and aero engine factories. The bombers sent to strike at these targets were well escorted by Bf 109Es from eight Jagdgeschwader, as the single-seat fighter force reached its peak strength. During 11 days of sustained

Spitfire IA X4179 of No. 19 Sqn is run up by its pilots shortly after being refuelled and re-armed at Fowlmere in early September 1940 – note the newly applied fabric patches covering the gun ports. This aircraft saw considerable action during the summer of 1940 with Nos 266, 19 and 609 Sqns.

attacks, which saw both sides suffer heavy losses, the Luftwaffe hoped to assert its dominance through sheer weight of numbers. Certainly the Luftwaffe enjoyed some success on Eagle Day and immediately afterwards, when a number of the more inexperienced RAF pilots were lost. However, all three of the major raids that day were picked up by radar and then intercepted. Although runways were damaged, they were quickly made operational again as the craters were filled in and key radar stations were always back up-and-running in a matter of hours. Eagle Day was designed to be the beginning of the end of Fighter Command. In this respect, the Luftwaffe did not even come close to success.

Between 24 August and 6 September, the Germans continued to target Fighter Command airfields and aircraft factories, with growing success. The RAF would later call this 'the critical period' of the Battle of Britain, as it found losses ever harder to replace, stretching the pilots and their aircraft to the limits of their endurance. Yet despite suffering serious casualties (136 Spitfires were lost in August alone), Fighter Command was in turn inflicting heavier losses on German forces. Indeed, Bf 110 *Zerstörer* (Destroyer) and Ju 87 Stuka Gruppen had been so badly affected that they would play little part in the rest of the campaign. Critically Reichsmarschall Hermann Göring questioned the tactics of continuing to attack radar stations when the British had so many, and he was also explicit in his order that airfields which 'had been successfully attacked one day should not be attacked the following day', presumably because he regarded it as a waste of effort. With this Göring virtually guaranteed the continued operational capabilities of the frontline Spitfire and Hurricane squadrons. German Bf 109 pilots' chances of winning the battle were therefore scuppered by the amateurish interference of Göring.

In contrast, British Spitfire pilots fell under the command of Air Chief Marshal Hugh Dowding. He had been responsible for introducing the 'Dowding system' whereby radar, raid plotting and radio control of aircraft were integrated. In the hands of this dedicated professional, ably assisted by Air Vice-Marshal Keith Park, commander of No. 11 Fighter Group, the British enjoyed a distinct advantage despite the scores of German bombers and fighters increasingly darkening the skies over south-east England.

His bombs gone, Unteroffizier Josef Heinzeller of 2./JG 3 races back across the Channel towards the Pas de Calais at low altitude in his distinctively marked Bf 109E-3/B. Protecting him on this Jabo mission, flown in late September, are two less elaborately marked Emils from the same Staffel. Heinzeller, who claimed five victories in 1940, named all of his aircraft after his pet dog, 'Schnauzl'.

On 7 September, believing that Fighter Command was finished, Reichsmarschall Göring ordered his forces to target London instead in an effort to bring more RAF fighters into the air. Eventually, the capital would be attacked both by day and night, culminating in two massive daylight raids (involving more than 250 bombers and 300+ Bf 109Es) on 15 September – immortalized thereafter by the British as Battle of Britain Day.

By now the Jagdflieger were forbidden to fly their favoured Freie Jagd sorties, ranging far and wide in front of the bombers. Instead, Reichsmarschall Göring ordered them to provide close formation escort for the bombers, which had suffered growing losses to the seemingly indestructible RAF. As if to prove that Fighter Command did indeed still have plenty of fight left in it, both waves of bombers were met by close to 300 Hurricanes and Spitfires. In what would prove to be one of the final large-scale raids made by the Luftwaffe during the campaign, 19 Bf 109Es were shot down. These aircraft were the last of nearly 400 Emils that had been lost or badly damaged in the four weeks from 13 August. Fighter Command lost seven Spitfires and 20 Hurricanes on 15 September.

On 30 September, the last massed daylight raids on London and the south-west were flown. Some 300 bombers attacked the capital in two waves, and the escorting 200 Bf 109Es suffered their worst losses of the Battle of Britain – 28 Emils were shot down, whilst the RAF lost 13 Hurricanes and four Spitfires.

Clearly Fighter Command was far from beaten, and Operation *Sealöwe* was shelved on 12 October. By then Göring had ordered that a third of all his Channel-based Jagdgeschwader strength had to be converted into fighter-bombers for 'tip-and-run' Jabo sorties due to the vulnerability of the medium bomber force in daylight raids. These missions were flown at high altitudes of between 26,000ft and 33,000ft, and Spitfire units struggled to intercept the Bf 109E Jabos. Conversely, little damage was done by the attacks, which were flown for nuisance value as much as anything else.

The Battle of Britain officially ended on 31 October, by which time 610 Bf 109Es had been lost in combat – a little more than one-third of the Luftwaffe's total losses of 1,792 aircraft. During the same period, Fighter Command had seen 361 of its Spitfires destroyed. Both the Spitfire I/II and the Bf 109E would continue to clash in the skies over England and, increasingly, occupied Europe through to the end of 1941, but the battle to prevent the fall of Britain, like the fall of France several months earlier, was over.

THE COMBATANTS

The majority of the single-seat fighter pilots that faced each other in 1940–41 were amongst the best trained aviators to see combat in World War II. This was particularly true for the Jagdflieger, many of whom had been flying with the Luftwaffe since its formation in the early 1930s. A significant number of Bf 109E pilots had also been blooded in Spain during the civil war, which had run from 1936 to 1939. Fighter tactics trialled and perfected in action against Republican aircraft influenced the way the Jagdwaffe trained and fought during the early years of World War II.

The pilots of RAF Fighter Command had no such combat experience, but they were very well trained nonetheless thanks to constant drilling and exercises. As detailed in the previous chapter, the ground control system in place in the UK was unmatched anywhere in the world, and fighter pilots were familiar with its operation.

As with the Jagdwaffe, Fighter Command only really began to feel the pinch in respect to the quality of the pilots reaching the front line during the latter stages of the Battle of Britain, when heavy losses forced Training Command to cut corners in order to keep units operational. By late 1940 the pilot crisis was over within the RAF, and training schemes both in the UK and overseas in southern Africa, Australia, the United States and Canada ensured that Fighter Command would never again suffer from a lack of personnel.

The same could not be said for the Jagdwaffe, however, which struggled to replace pilots lost as the war progressed. Although losses in 1940 were swiftly made good, poor organization of its training units eventually resulted in serious pilot shortages from 1943 onwards.

BRIAN JOHN GEORGE CARBURY

The RAF's leading Spitfire ace during the Battle of Britain, and also the only pilot in Fighter Command to down five Bf 109Es in a single day during 1940, Brian Carbury was born in Wellington, New Zealand, on 27 February 1918. A giant of a man at 6ft 4in., he was also a fine sportsman and an excellent marksman. Following brief employment as a shoe salesman in Auckland, he travelled to England in June 1937 and secured a short-service commission in the RAF after being turned down by the Royal Navy for being too old. Undertaking his flying training at No. 10 E&RFTS, Carbury was eventually posted to No. 41 Sqn at Catterick in June 1938, where he flew Fury II biplanes.

His unit converted to Spitfire Is in January 1939, and in October of that same year he was temporarily reassigned to No. 603 'City of Edinburgh' Sqn at Turnhouse to help with its transition from Gladiators to Spitfires. He was permanently assigned to the auxiliary squadron upon the outbreak of war and saw his first action in December 1939 when he damaged an He 111 near Arbroath. Carbury followed this up with a share in the destruction of a second Heinkel bomber off Aberdeen on 7 March 1940 and a Ju 88 near Montrose on 3 July.

On 28 August No. 603 Sqn was sent south from Scotland to Hornchurch to relieve battle-weary Spitfire unit No. 65 Sqn. In the coming weeks the unit would claim 67 German aircraft destroyed for the loss of 30 Spitfires. Four of its pilots would also claim five or more Bf 109Es destroyed. Carbury emerged as the unit's ace of aces, downing eight Emils during the first week of No. 603 Sqn's operations with No. 11 Group. Five of these came during the course of three sorties on 31 August, thus making him one of only two Fighter Command aces in a day during the Battle of Britain (the other was No. 610 Sqn's Sgt Ronnie Hamlyn, who claimed four Bf 109Es and a Ju 88 on 24 August).

Carbury was awarded a DFC and Bar in September and October 1940, and by year-end his tally stood at 15 and two shared destroyed, two probables and five damaged. Like many pre-war fighter pilots to survive the Battle of Britain, he was posted as an instructor to Training

Command in December 1940, joining No. 58 OTU. Carbury remained an instructor until dismissed from the service in 1944 following a court martial for bouncing cheques that had been written to cover his wife's opulent lifestyle. He had his British pilot's licence suspended in 1948 for ferrying aircraft to Israel (which was not allowed at the time), and eventually found work as a salesman for a heating firm. Carbury was diagnosed with terminal acute monocytic leukaemia and died on 31 July 1961.

New Zealander Al Deere was one of many short-service commission officers to join the RAF during its period of rapid expansion in the late 1930s. Like a number of these pre-war recruits from 'the Dominions', he would enjoy great success in the Spitfire in 1940–41.

BRITISH PILOT TRAINING

The RAF was blighted by a lack of funding from 1919 until 1936, when the overt re-arming of Germany prompted the government of the day to at last provide funding that would allow the air force to carry out its duties effectively in a modern war. Central to this re-equipment was the purchase of new single-seat monoplane fighters in the shape of the Hurricane and Spitfire. A large number of pilots would be needed to fly these aircraft in the front line, and it was obvious that the existing Flying Training Schools (for short-service commission officers and airmen pilots) and RAF College training (for permanent officers) output of around 400 pilots a year was grossly inadequate.

As part of the shake up of the RAF instigated by the Air Ministry in 1936, which saw four specialist commands created in place of the Area Commands that had previously existed, Training Command was established. Three years prior to this change, the RAF had already taken steps to improve the volume of its pilot training by establishing a handful of civilian-manned Elementary and Reserve Flying Training Schools (E&RFTSs), equipped with Gipsy Moths, Tiger Moths and Blackburn B 2s. It had also established a standardized training programme for future officer pilots at the RAF College at Cranwell that same year.

Coinciding with the formation of Training Command, the Air Ministry had created the RAF Volunteer Reserve (RAFVR) to train 800 pilots a year. Open to all comers, no matter what their financial or social status, this scheme proved so popular that by 1940 a third of Fighter Command's pilots had joined as RAFVRs – a considerable number were posted to frontline units as sergeant pilots. Prior to this, all recruits entered either as permanent or short-commission officers and NCOs, or via the Auxiliary Air Force (AAF). The latter, created in 1925, mirrored the Territorial Army in that units consisted of groups of men from particular areas who trained together at weekends. These squadrons were quickly manned by wealthy gentlemen, who set the tone for the auxiliaries into the early stages of World War II.

By late 1938, close to 30 E&RFTSs had been established, setting student pilots on the path to obtaining their wings through training on Tiger Moths, Magisters and

B 2s. An element of advanced training had also been introduced at these schools through the provision of Harts, Battles and Ansons.

Amongst the pilots to experience the RAF's revised pilot training was future Spitfire ace Al Deere, who was one of 12 New Zealanders selected to travel to the UK in September 1937 – many young men from across the Empire took up short-service commissions in the air force during this period. Deere was initially sent to the de Havilland Civil School of Flying at White Waltham, where he underwent an *ab initio* flying course for the next three months prior to being accepted into the RAF. Towards the end of this initial training phase, pilots were asked to make a choice as to whether they wanted to fly bombers or fighters – Deere, of course, chose the latter.

Following graduation from the E&RFTS, pilots destined to be commissioned then spent two weeks undergoing officer training at RAF Uxbridge, where they were fitted with uniforms, prior to heading to a Flying Training School (FTS). Deere went to No. 6 FTS at Netheravon, in Wiltshire, where he flew Hart biplanes in his junior term. Upon completion of this phase of his training, he was awarded his pilots' Wings, after which he flew Fury biplane fighters (then still very much in service with Fighter Command) during his senior term. Completing his nine months of flying training in August 1938, Deere was duly posted to Hornchurch, in No. 11 Group, to fly Gladiators with No. 54 Sqn.

Like most pre-war fighter pilots already serving with frontline or auxiliary units, Al Deere made the transition from biplane to monoplane at squadron level, as there were insufficient Spitfires and Hurricanes available to supply them to Training Command. Most pilots had plenty of flying experience under their belts by the time the switch was made, and the change in types posed few problems, as Deere noted in his autobiography, *Nine Lives*:

> On 6 March 1939, I flew my first Spitfire. The transition from slow biplanes to the faster monoplanes was effected without fuss, and in a matter of weeks we were nearly as

A 'vic' of No. 65 Sqn Spitfire IAs scramble from RAF Hornchurch on 13 August 1940 – the day the Luftwaffe officially launched its all-out assault on military targets in England, code-named *Adlerangriff*. No. 65 Sqn was using RAF Manston, on the Kent coast, as its forward airfield at the time, and was already on patrol when the station was badly bombed that day. During its 15 days of combat in the Battle of Britain, No. 65 Sqn claimed 31 victories (of which only 10.5 can be confirmed with any accuracy) and lost 15 Spitfires.

competent on Spitfires as we had been on Gladiators. Training on Spitfires followed the same pattern as on Gladiators, except that we did a little more cine-gun work to get practice on the new reflector gunsight with which the aircraft was fitted.

Fighter Command did, however, try to fill the obvious performance gap between an obsolescent biplane fighter or Harvard advanced trainer flown by a brand new pilot in an FTS and the monoplane fighter that awaited him in the frontline. It established several Group Pools in 1939 and equipped them with a handful of Hurricanes and Spitfires. New pilots would now be able to get a precious few flying hours in their logbooks on-type before joining Fighter Command proper.

With the declaration of war, all E&RFTSs were brought within the RAF Training Command structure as Elementary Flying Training Schools (EFTSs). Once finished here, pupils would then progress to Service Flying Training Schools (SFTSs), boosted in number from six to eleven by early 1940. The types operated at both stages in the training process remained much the same during the first 18 months of the war, although the inter-war biplane fighters seen at the SFTSs slowly began to be replaced by more Harvards and the all-new Miles Master.

The Group Pool system, from which operational squadrons were able to draw replacement pilots, and thus relinquish their own training responsibilities so as to concentrate on performing combat missions, soon showed signs of failure in wartime. Indeed, literally thousands of trainee pilots (many with considerable flying hours) were transferred into other trades in late 1939 and early 1940 because of a chronic shortage of monoplane fighter types within the Group Pools. Spitfires and Hurricanes were urgently needed in the front line, leaving none for training purposes. In the spring of 1940, all Group Pools were redesignated Operational Training Units (OTUs) within Training Command, and the Air Ministry instructed Fighter Command to make sure that sufficient aircraft were made available to these units so that a steady flow of replacement pilots could be sent through them. The OTUs eventually succeeded where the Group Pools had failed thanks to an influx of combat-weary fighters and equally battle-seasoned staff to instruct would-be frontline pilots.

When losses began to mount in August 1940, OTU courses for new pilots were drastically cut in length from several months to just four weeks, leaving squadrons to apply the finishing touches. As a result of this, Fighter Command began receiving replacement pilots who had not yet mastered the Spitfire or Hurricane, and who had received little more than basic training in blind or night flying, navigation or gunnery – indeed, a number of pilots had never fired their guns at all prior to engaging the enemy for the first time.

Despite cutting corners in pilot training, still more pilots were needed as replacements as the Luftwaffe continued to exact a heavy toll on the RAF. With no time to train them from scratch, Fighter Command sought out pilots from other commands within the RAF, as well as from the Fleet Air Arm – the best pilots from Army Cooperation, Coastal and Bomber Commands were posted in, as were 75 partly trained naval pilots. Combat-seasoned fighter pilots also came from Poland, Czechoslovakia, Belgium and France, having fled to Britain following the German

HERBERT IHLEFELD

Although credited with more Spitfire I/IIs destroyed than any other Bf 109E pilot, Herbert Ihlefeld, uniquely, claimed all of these victories flying with a mixed-formation *Lehrgeschwader* (training wing) tasked with the development of new tactics, rather than an out and out fighter Jagdgeschwader. Born in Pinnow, Pomerania, on 1 June 1914, Ihlefeld was an original member of the Jadgwaffe upon its formation in 1933. Following service with the Jagdgeschwader JG 132 'Richthofen', where he flew He 51s and the all-new Bf 109B-1, Ihlefeld volunteered for duty with the Condor Legion in late 1937.

Assigned to 2./J 88 upon his arrival in Spain, Feldwebel Ihlefeld's previous flying experience with the Messerschmitt fighter stood him in good stead, and he was issued with one of the first Bf 109B-1s to arrive in-theatre. His unit saw much action during the Aragón offensive in the spring and summer of 1938, and Ihlefeld finished his tour with nine victories to his credit. Returning to Germany in 1939 with the rank of Leutnant, he was posted to the newly formed Lehrgeschwader 2 at Garz, whose I Gruppe was equipped with Bf 109Ds. This Geschwader was the second Operational Instruction and Evaluation Group to be formed by the Luftwaffe, and I.(J)/LG 2 was its fighter component, equipped with 45 Bf 109Es by the autumn of 1939. Leutnant Ihlefeld was attached to the Stab of this unit, and saw action in Poland and during the Blitzkrieg in the West.

He claimed his first success – a French Morane-Saulnier MS.406 fighter – on 29 May 1940, and followed this up with an RAF Blenheim and a Spitfire on 30 June after I.(J)/LG 2's move to Marquise, in the Pas de Calais. The latter aircraft would be the first of no fewer than 33 Spitfire I/IIs victories credited to Ihlefeld between the end of June 1940 and 23 March 1941. Made Gruppenkommandeur of I.(J)/LG 2 on 30 August 1940, Hauptmann Ihlefeld downed no fewer than 15 Spitfires in September alone, being awarded the Knight's Cross that same month.

His success against the RAF's best fighters ended in April 1941 when he led his unit to the Balkans to participate in the invasion of Yugoslavia. Ironically, Ihlefeld's Bf 109E-7 was shot down by groundfire on the

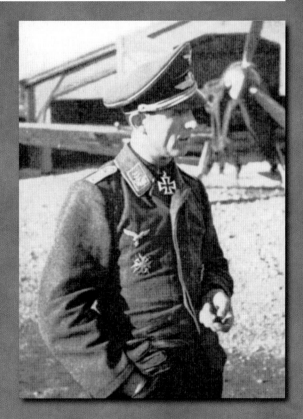

opening day of Operation *Marita* and he spent several days as a PoW. The I.(J)/LG 2 duly participated in Operation *Barbarossa* as I Gruppe of JG 77 from the very start of the offensive, and Ihlefeld, who eventually joined the Stab of I./JG 77 in late 1941, scored heavily in the first ten months of the campaign and duly became only the fifth pilot in the Jagdwaffe to reach the 100-kill mark, attained on 22 April 1942. By then Gruppenkommandeur of I./JG 77, he then became Geschwaderkommodore of JG 52, again in the east, on 22 June 1942.

Ihlefeld, eventually promoted to the rank of Oberst, would subsequently lead JGs 103 (a fighter training unit), 25, 11 and 1, scoring his final 13 victories during Defence of the Reich operations in 1944. He was also awarded the Oak Leaves and Swords to his Knight's Cross. Ihlefeld survived the war as the last Geschwaderkommodore of JG 1, having completed more than 1,000 combat missions and having scored 123 aerial victories in World War II.

occupation of their respective countries. These were the men that manned the 19 Spitfire squadrons that helped defend Britain in the summer of 1940.

GERMAN PILOT TRAINING

Prior to the official creation of the Luftwaffe, all air activity in Germany had been geared towards training because of the ban on military flying under the terms of the 1919 Treaty of Versailles. Those quasi-military aviation organizations that were formed in Germany during the late 1920s and early 1930s functioned under the cover of civilian activities. Although the restrictions stalled the development of both combat aircraft and tactics, the focus on flying training provided the newly formed Luftwaffe with plenty of military-trained aircrew. Men came from Lufthansa, gliding clubs and, until 1936, the army. However, the latter was expanding rapidly too, and senior officers forbade the Luftwaffe from recruiting from within the Wehrmacht. Conscripts and volunteers would make up the numbers from then on.

Obsolete fighters such as the He 51 were put to good use by would-be Jagdflieger during their three to four months of advanced tuition in Jagdfliegervorschulen or Waffenschule, prior to being sent to Erganzungsgruppen (Operational Training Schools) for the teaching of tactics and further familiarization with more modern frontline types such as the Bf 109E.

In Germany, pilot recruitment and training was strongly influenced by Prussian military tradition. Initially, all future officers and NCOs alike could expect to undertake six months of labour service, organized in a paramilitary fashion, with the *Reichsarbeitdienst* (Reich Labour Service). Those that were particularly air-minded chose service with the Party-controlled *Nationalsozialistisches Fliegerkorps* (National Socialist Flyers' Corp) instead, flying gliders. However, with the Luftwaffe desperately short of personnel, labour service was reduced to just three months.

Induction into the Luftwaffe then followed, after which all recruits spent between six and twelve months undertaking basic infantry training at a *Flieger-Ersatzabteilung* (flying replacement unit). Once deemed to be effective infantrymen, all recruits were reviewed for possible advancement as pilots. Likely candidates were sent to a *Flug-Anwärterkompanie* (aircrew candidate company) for evaluation in a series of tests in basic aviation theory.

Most Jagdflieger flying Bf 109Es in 1939–40 would have gone through the full Luftwaffe training course. However, from late 1940 onwards, with the growing demand for pilots following the commencement of World War II, training and recruiting staff rationalized and compressed the initial stages of aircrew selection to enable trainees to embark upon the most appropriate training regime more expeditiously. The Flieger-Ersatzabteilung was now replaced by a series of *Flieger-Ausbildungsregiments* (flyer training regiments), where recruits would receive basic military training and preliminary aviation instruction. Potential pilots were then sent to undergo the standard selection process within a Flug-Anwärterkompanie, where the rest of their basic training, conducted over a period of three–four months, was completed alongside the aircrew evaluation tests.

Upon assignment to a Flug-Anwärterkompanie, the *Flugzeugführer-Anwärter* (pilot candidate) would receive instruction in basic flight theory and rudimentary

A veteran of service defending the Fatherland with I./JG 1 (note the Geschwader badge below the cockpit), this Bf 109E-4/B served with Ergänzungsgruppe JG 54 at Cazaux, on the west coast of France, in 1942. It was one of a number of obsolescent Emils to find employment as pilot trainers several years after the Battle of Britain. Note that the aircraft has been fitted with a bomb rack so that student pilots could use it to practise Jabo tactics.

BF 109E-4 COCKPIT

1. Machine gun firing button
2. Control column
3. Rudder pedal
4. Fuel cock
5. FuG VII radio control switch
6. Fuel contents gauge
7. Cockpit light control
8. Pitot head-heating warning lamp
9. Circuit breaker
10. Airspeed indicator
11. Engine starter switch
12. Turn and bank indicator
13. Altimeter
14. Compass

15. Instructions for flap settings, landing speed, etc.
16. Clock
17. Revi C/12D gunsight
18. Boost gauge
19. Compass deviation table
20. Tachometer
21. Propeller pitch indicator
22. Undercarriage position indicator
23. Fuel and oil pressure gauge
24. Undercarriage control lever
25. Undercarriage emergency control lever

26. Mechanical undercarriage position indicator
27. Filter pump control lever
28. Coolant temperature gauge
29. Oil temperature gauge
30. Low fuel warning lamp
31. Elevator control wheel
32. Landing flap control
33. Oil cooler flap control
34. Throttle control
35. Main instrument light
36. Engine instant-stop lever
37. Engine ignition lever
38. Starter coupling lever

39. Canopy release lever
40. Seat height adjustment lever
41. Tailplane incidence indicator
42. Circuit breaker panel
43. Oxygen hose
44. Main instrument light
45. Radiator flap control
46. Fuel pump auto switch
47. Map holder
48. Pilot's seat
49. Seat harness adjustment lever
50. Fuel injection pump
51. Remote control ventilator
52. Oxygen apparatus

SPITFIRE I/II COCKPIT

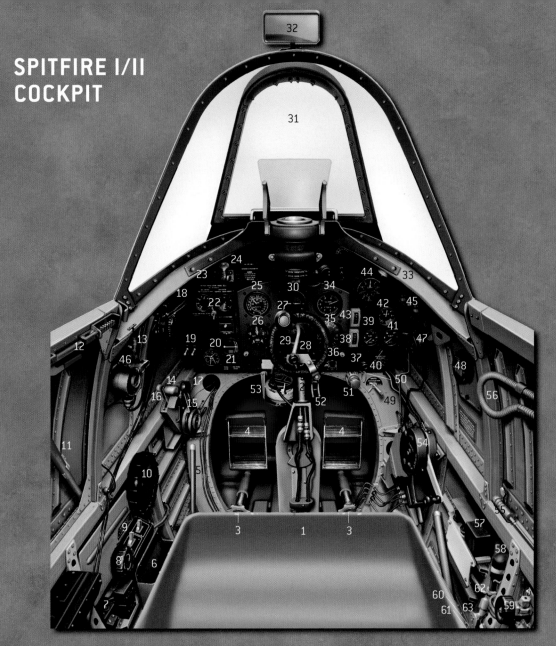

1. Seat
2. Control column
3. Rudder pedal adjusting wheel
4. Rudder pedal
5. Radiator flap control lever
6. Map case
7. Oil dilution push button
8. Rudder trim wheel
9. Pressure head heater switch
10. Elevator trim wheel
11. Crowbar
12. Door catch
13. Camera indication supply plug
14. Mixture lever
15. Throttle lever
16. Propeller control lever
17. Boost control cut-out

18. Radio controller
19. Ignition switch
20. Brake triple pressure gauge
21. Elevator tabs position indicator
22. Oxygen regulator
23. Navigation lights switch
24. Flaps control
25. Airspeed indicator
26. Altimeter
27. Gun button
28. Cockpit light switches
29. Direction indicator setting knob
30. Artificial horizon
31. GM 2 reflector gunsight
32. Rearview mirror
33. Ventilator control
34. Rate of climb indicator

35. Turn and slip indicator
36. Booster coil pushbutton
37. Engine starting pushbutton
38. Oil pressure gauge
39. Oil temperature gauge
40. Fuel gauge and pushbutton
41. Radiator temperature gauge
42. Boost pressure gauge
43. Fuel pressure warning lamp
44. Engine rpms
45. Stowage for reflector sight lamp
46. Cockpit light
47. Signalling switchbox
48. Remote contactor and switch
49. Fuel tank pressurizing cock control
50. Slow running cut-out control

51. Priming pump
52. Fuel cock
53. Compass
54. Undercarriage control lever
55. Harness release
56. Oxygen hose
57. IFF Controls
58. CO2 cylinder for undercarriage emergency lowering
59. Oxygen supply cock
60. Windscreen de-icing pump
61. Windscreen de-icing needle valve
62. Undercarriage emergency lowering control
63. Windscreen de-icing cock

aeronautics in aircraft such as the Bü 131, Ar 66C, He 72 Kaddett, Go 145 and Fw 44 Stieglitz biplane trainers. Assessed for advancement throughout this phase, those candidates displaying the required aptitude were then sent to Flugzeugführerschule A/B (Pilot School A/B) as soon as a space became available – typically two months after arriving at the Flug-Anwärterkompanie. Here, flight training proper would be undertaken.

At such schools, students underwent four principal levels of instruction, each requiring qualification for its own licence, before advancing to the next stage. These licences, earned over a period of six to nine months, gave the schools their name. The *A1-Schien* introduced students to basic practical flying in dual-controlled training aircraft, the instructors teaching recruits how to take off and land, recover from stalls and attain their solo flight rating. Pre-war and through to early 1941, instructors would have been assigned four trainees each – this number rose as the conflict progressed.

At the *A2-Schien*, cadets were required to learn the theory of flight, including aerodynamics, meteorology, flying procedures and aviation law, as well as the practical application of aeronautical engineering, elementary navigation, wireless procedure and Morse code. In the air, they gained more flying experience on larger single-engine two-seat aircraft.

The next level of training, known as the *B1-Schien*, saw pilots progress onto high-performance single- and twin-engined machines typically fitted with a retractable undercarriage – if destined to fly fighters, older types of combat aircraft such as early Bf 109s would be flown for the first time. Precision landings, night flying and cross-country flying were all tested in this phase of the course. The student pilot would also have to complete at least 50 flights in a B1 category aircraft. Upon graduation from the *B1-Schien*, students would then undertake training aimed at acquiring the final *B2-Schien*, having accumulated 100 to 150 hours of flight time over the previous 14 to 17 months.

In late 1940 the Flugzeugführerschule A/B was streamlined to take into account wartime demand for pilots, with a far greater emphasis now being placed on practical flying skills from the outset. The A2 licence was dropped, with that phase being amalgamated into the remaining grades. The A licence generally took three months to complete, with the B phase seeing pilots flying more advanced types. An elementary K1 *Kunstflug* (stunt-flying) aerobatics course was also included in the latter phase to provide all pilots with a good understanding of rudimentary evasive manoeuvres (barrel rolls, loops and formation splits). This phase also allowed instructors to identify any potential fighter pilots among their students, who thereafter received more flying time than their fellow students.

Upon completion of the B2 phase, the cadet would finally be granted his *Luftwaffeflugzeugführerschein* (air force pilots' licence), accompanied by the highly prized *Flugzeugführerabzeichen* (pilot's badge) – his 'wings'. After an average of ten to 13 months at Flugzeugführerschule A/B, he was now a fully qualified pilot.

It was at this point that new pilots were categorized for service on single- or multi-engined aircraft, with each being assigned to a specialist flying school. Here each pilot would undergo intensive training for his allotted aircraft type, with potential fighter pilots being sent directly to *Jagdfliegervorschulen* (fighter school) or *Waffenschule* (military school) for three to four months, where they carried out 50 hours of flying on semi-obsolescent types. For Bf 109E pilots this usually meant Ar 68 and He 51 biplanes, Bf 109B/C/Ds and Ar 96s. By the time he was eventually posted to a frontline unit, a pilot could expect to have 200 hours of flying time under his belt. Officer candidates would have also attended *Luftkriegschule* (air war school) to learn tactics, air force law and military discipline, prior to their assignment to a Jagdfliegervorschulen.

The realities of war led the Luftwaffe to further modify the final stages of its training syllabus in 1940, with the creation of *Erganzungsgruppen* (operational training schools) for the teaching of tactics and further familiarization with frontline types. In the Jagdwaffe, these units were directly linked to and controlled by operational Geschwader. Designated IV Gruppe, these units were intended to allow new pilots to gain precious operational experience before being hurled into combat.

Surviving Bf 109Es soldiered on with Erganzungsgruppen, and the three Fighter Pools that replaced them in the summer of 1942, well into 1943.

COMBAT

The first documented action between an armed Spitfire I and a Bf 109E took place just south of Calais late in the morning of 23 May 1940. With things going badly for the Allies, Prime Minister Winston Churchill had ordered that more Fighter Command squadrons be moved to France. Air Chief Marshal Dowding strongly resisted this order, instead ordering six No. 11 Group units to be moved to forward airfields along the south coast.

A number of squadrons previously not involved in the Battle of France would commence operations along the French coast from 16 May, including Spitfire-equipped Nos 54 and 74 Sqns which were now ordered to provide fighter cover and support for Allied forces withdrawing to the Dunkirk region from the Low Countries.

On the morning of 23 May, Spitfires from No. 74 Sqn had engaged a Henschel Hs 126 observation aircraft and shot it down. However, defensive fire from the aircraft had hit the radiator of one of the fighters and forced its pilot, Sqn Ldr F. L. White, to land at nearby Calais-Marck airfield. The latter was under threat by advancing German troops, so it was decided that a rescue mission needed to be sent, involving a two-seat Master and two escorting Spitfires from No. 54 Sqn. Flying the latter were future aces Plt Offs Johnny Allen (who would later be killed in action by Hauptmann Adolf Galland on 24 July 1940 – the first Spitfire downed by the German ace) and Al Deere.

Once over the French airfield, they were engaged by a number of Bf 109Es from I./JG 27. With the Master safely on the ground, the two Spitfire pilots engaged the German fighters and claimed three destroyed. Al Deere later recalled:

This was my first real combat, and the first recorded combat of a Spitfire with a Bf 109. My abiding memory was the thrill of the action – there was no sense of danger at that early stage in the war. So much so that I stayed behind the second of the two Bf 109s that

I encountered after I had run out of ammunition just to see if I could do so. I only broke off when petrol became a factor. My prolonged fight with this Bf 109 allowed me to assess the relative performance of the two aircraft.

In early engagements between the Hurricane and Bf 109 in France, the speed and climb of the latter had become legendary, and were claimed by many to be far superior to that of the Spitfire. I was able to refute this, and indeed was confident that, except in a dive, the Spitfire was superior in most other fields, and was vastly more manoeuvrable. My superior rate of climb was, however, due mostly to the type of Spitfire with which my squadron was equipped. We had the first Rotol constant-speed airscrews on which we had been doing trials when the fighting started. Other Spitfires were, at that stage, using a two-speed airscrew (either fully fine pitch or fully course), which meant they lost performance in a climb. The constant-speed unit changed its pitch as the engine revs went up.

There was a great deal of scepticism about my claim that the Spitfire was the superior fighter, but the big thing for me was that we shouldn't have any fear of the Bf 109 in combat.

Although this was the first recorded clash in combat between the Spitfire and Bf 109, it was not the first time that these machines had come up against one another in the air. On 22 November 1939, Bf 109E-3 Wk-Nr 1304 of 1./JG 76 was landed intact at Strasbourg-Woerth airfield in France by Feldwebel Karl Hier after he had become disorientated in thick fog. His Emil was thoroughly tested by the Armée de l'Air, after which it was flown to the UK in May 1940 for trials at the RAE at Farnborough.

In a series of mock combats fought between the German fighter and a Spitfire I fitted with a two-speed airscrew (most constant-speed units were being allocated to bombers at the time, although this would change during the early summer of 1940), the Bf 109E was found to be superior in all aspects bar its manoeuvrability and turning circle. The margins reduced rapidly when the Spitfire was fitted with a constant-speed airscrew, however, as Al Deere proved over France later that month.

In level flight, the Spitfire had little trouble staying behind the Bf 109E, nor did a dive present the pursuer with many problems. However, when the Messerschmitt was pulled out of the dive and into a steep climb at slow speeds, the Spitfire pilot had difficulty in following the German fighter. When the Spitfire was being pursued in a turning fight at medium altitude, the trials proved that the RAF fighter was the superior aircraft. Thanks to

The RAF's standard formation of three-aircraft 'vics' proved to be inflexible when Fighter Command encountered the Jagdwaffe in 1940. The fighters flew so close together that only the lead pilot had time to search for the enemy, with the remaining 11 having to focus on their formation flying.

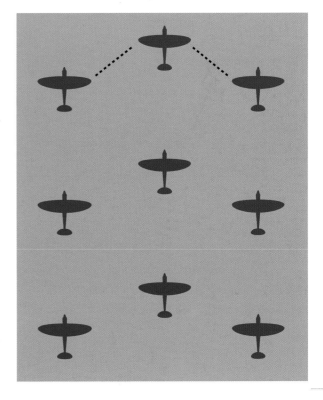

its outstanding rate of roll, the Spitfire pilot could shake off the Bf 109E by performing a flick half-roll and quickly pulling out of the subsequent dive. The Messerschmitt pilot found it difficult to counter this defensive manoeuvre because his elevators became too heavy to effect a quick pull out due to the fighter's rapid build up of speed in the dive. An experienced German pilot could, however, remain on the Spitfire's tail throughout this manoeuvre if the latter was flown by a novice who failed to tighten his turn for fear of stalling his fighter.

During the course of the trial it was discovered that a Bf 109E pilot could also push his aircraft into a sudden dive in an effort to elude a pursuing Spitfire, and the German fighter's DB 601 engine would continue to deliver full power thanks to its direct fuel injection. However, if a Spitfire tried to follow, its Merlin engine would splutter and stop because its normal float-type carburettor ceased to deliver fuel. RAF pilots quickly learned to half-roll and pull down in pursuit of a bunting Bf 109E, thus negating the fuel flow problems.

The Bf 109E drew praise from the RAF trials team for its excellent handling and low- and medium-speed response, good low-speed climb angle, gentle stall, lack of any tendency to spin and short take-off run. However, it was criticized for its control heaviness at the upper end of its speed range – the Spitfire was just as difficult to fly at around 400mph, losing any clear advantage in manoeuvrability that it enjoyed over the Bf 109E. Indeed, German pilots soon discovered in combat that if they kept their speed up, and flew evasively, the Spitfire pilot would struggle to bring his guns to bear. The absence of a rudder trimmer in the Bf 109E was also noted by the RAF trials pilots, who grew weary of constantly having to apply the rudder in order to fly

Bf 109E-3 Wk-Nr 1304 was landed in error by its pilot in northern France in November 1939, and following flight trials with the Armée de l'Air, the fighter was handed over to the RAF. Repainted in full RAF colours, the aircraft was extensively evaluated by the Experimental Flying Department at RAE Farnborough in May and June 1940, when it completed 53 flights against all manner of frontline RAF types. Eventually sent to the USA in January 1942 for further flight trials, this much-travelled Emil was damaged beyond repair in a forced landing in Ohio on 3 November that same year.

straight at high speeds. They also commented unfavourably on the Bf 109E's uncomfortably cramped cockpit.

Dr Alfred Price, when commenting on the results of this trial in his volume *Spitfire At War*, noted:

Overall, the Spitfire I and Bf 109E matched each other fairly evenly. If they fought, victory would almost invariably go to the side which was the more alert, which held the initiative, which understood the strengths and weaknesses of its opponent's aircraft, which showed better team work and which, in the last resort, could shoot the more accurately.

The fall of France in June 1940 also presented the Luftwaffe with the opportunity to test-fly a Spitfire after three examples were captured on the ground. Amongst the pilots to evaluate the captured Spitfire at the Luftwaffe's Rechlin test centre was then ranking German ace (with 39 kills, including 14 in Spain) Hauptmann Werner Mölders, who flew both the Spitfire and the Hurricane. Writing to his comrades in III./JG 53 about his Rechlin experiences, Mölders noted:

In our terms, both British fighters are easy to fly... Take-off and landing in both types is child's play… The Spitfire is one class better [than the Hurricane], being very nice to the touch, light, excellent in the turn and almost equal to the Bf 109E in performance, but a rotten dogfighter, as any sudden dive and the engine cuts out for seconds at a time, and because the propeller's only two-pitch (take-off and cruise), it means that in any vertical dogfight at constantly changing heights it's either continually over-revving or never develops full power at all.

Fellow ace Oberleutnant Erwin Leykauf (who survived the war with 33 kills to his credit) of 7./JG 54 was also quite candid about the capabilities of the Spitfires he encountered during the summer of 1940, recalling in Armand van Ishoven's *Messerschmitt Bf 109 At War* volume:

Spitfire Is of No. 19 Sqn head away from Fowlmere in 1940 in tight Battle Formation. The rigid adherence to such unwieldy tactics by the RAF saw Spitfire and Hurricane units sustain heavy losses to marauding Bf 109Es during the Battle of Britain.

Next page:
At 1630hrs on 30 August 1940, No. 603 Sqn's Flg Off Brian Carbury was leading a section in B Flight when, near Canterbury, he sighted three Bf 109s north of him. 'I attacked the rear aircraft, and the leading two aircraft turned for my tail. I got a good burst in and the propeller of the rear enemy aircraft stopped, started and finally stopped, with white vapour coming out behind. The enemy aircraft went into a glide for the east coast. I veered off as other aircraft were closing in on me.' The Bf 109E-1 of 3./JG 27's Feldwebel Ernst Arnold had been badly shot up, but its pilot managed to perform a controlled belly landing in a field near Faversham.

The remains of No. 65 Sqn Spitfire I K9912 sit abandoned on the beach at Dunkirk following its force-landing by Plt Off Ken Hart on 26 May 1940. Just moments prior to his fighter being mortally damaged in combat with a Bf 109E, future ace Hart had claimed his first victory when he had downed an Emil. Having set fire to his Spitfire, Hart returned to the UK by ship two days later. K9912 was just one of 61 Spitfires lost in combat by the RAF between 22 May and 2 June 1940.

The essential difference between the Bf 109E and the Spitfire I was that the latter was less manoeuvrable in the rolling plane. With its shorter, square-tipped wings, the Bf 109E was more manoeuvrable and slightly faster. It also had leading edge slots. When the Bf 109 was flown, advertently or inadvertently, too slow, the slots would shoot out forward of the wing... Many fresh young pilots thought that they were pulling very tight turns even when the slots were closed against the wing. For us more experienced pilots, real maneuvering only started when the slots were out. For this reason, it is possible to find pilots from 1940 who will tell you that the Spitfire turned better than the Bf 109... I myself had many dogfights with Spitfires and could always out-turn them.

In light of the combat experiences over Dunkirk and in the early stages of the Battle of Britain, the RAF rapidly fitted Rotol variable-pitch propellers to all of its Spitfire in frontline units, thus allowing the fighter to match the performance of the Bf 109E.

BRITISH TACTICS

As good as the Spitfire was, its employment in the first 18 months of the war was adversely affected by the rigid implementation of unwieldy tactics. In the 1930s the greatest perceived threat was from the bomber. Given the range of fighters, and the fact that France was an ally, it was assumed that the bombers would be unescorted. However, RAF fighters were armed exclusively with rifle-calibre 0.303-in. machine guns at this time, and their weight of fire was deemed to be insufficient to bring down bombers flying in tight, massed formations when attacking independently of one another. The RAF's Air Fighting Development Establishment (AFDE) therefore decided that the only way to solve this problem was to mass fighters in close formation so as to bring a large number of guns to bear. Pilots in frontline fighter units were well drilled in formation flying, so a series of six basic patterns known as

Fighting Area Attacks were duly formulated and published in the RAF Manual of Air Tactics of 1938. These were at the heart of standard squadron air drills, as Al Deere recalled:

> The majority of our training in a pre-war fighter squadron was directed at achieving perfection in formation, with a view to ensuring the success of the flight and the squadron attacks we so assiduously practised. The order to attack was always preceded by the flight commander designating the number of the attack, such as 'Fighting Area Attack No. 5 – Go'. These attacks provided wonderful training for formation drill, but were worthless when related to effective shooting. There was never sufficient time to get one's sights on the target, the business of keeping station being the prime requirement.

The standard RAF fighter formation at the time was the V-shaped 'vic' of three aircraft. A squadron of 12 aircraft would be split into two flights, A and B, and these were in turn made up of two sections of three fighters. When in full-strength Battle Formation, all 12 aircraft would be tightly grouped together in four sections of three fighters. Leading the 'vic' would be the squadron CO or senior flight commander, with succeeding 'Vs' following in close line astern. Once bombers had been spotted, the commander would position his formation in behind them and then lead the attack in section after section. Such attacks would have worked well against German bombers had it not been for the presence of agile escort fighters sweeping the skies ahead of them. As RAF Fighter Command would soon find out to its cost, Fighting Area Attacks (FAAs) were useless against small, nimble formations of high performance fighters such as the Bf 109E. Indeed, upon seeing British fighters flying into combat in tight, neat rows of three, German pilots, who invariably enjoyed a height advantage, quickly dubbed the 'vics' *Idiotenreihen* (lit. 'rows of idiots').

Those pilots that survived their initial encounters with the enemy soon came to realize that a successful combat formation had to be able to manoeuvre whilst maintaining cohesion. Pilots also had to be able to cover each other's blind areas so as

No. 610 'County of Chester' Sqn carry out a Channel patrol from Gravesend in early June 1940. The unit had seen much action over France during Operation *Dynamo*, and lessons learned during this period are reflected in the loose line-astern formations flown by two of three sections seen in this view. Subsequently in action for 20 days during the Battle of Britain, No. 610 Sqn would claim 58 victories (of which 30.5 can be credited). More than half of these kills were Bf 109Es. The unit lost 20 Spitfires in return.

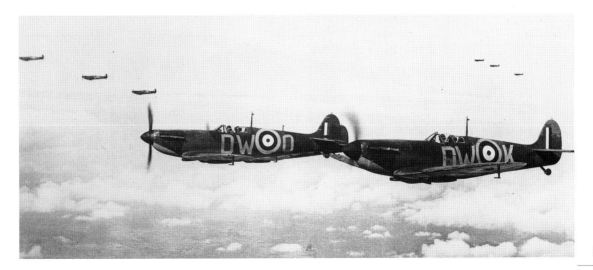

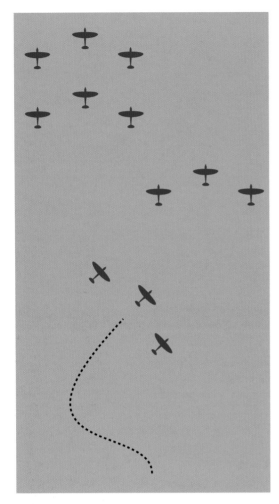

to prevent surprise attacks on the formation. Finally, individual members of the formation had to be able to support each other should they come under attack.

The Luftwaffe's four-strong Schwarm (based on the loose pair, or Rotte, which was at the heart of all Jagdwaffe formations) meet all these criteria, but Fighter Command's tight 'vics' did not. The Schwarm could turn as tightly as any individual aircraft within the formation, whereas the 'vic's' rate of turn was limited by the need for it to pivot on the aircraft on the inside of the turn.

When looking for the enemy, all the members of the looser Schwarm enjoyed the freedom to search the skies (and cover blind areas astern of the formation) without the fear of running into a wingman. In the 'vic', only the leader searched for the enemy, as his two wingmen had to concentrate on remaining in tight formation. This left them highly susceptible to attack from behind and below, and this blind spot was repeatedly exploited by the Jagdwaffe in 1940.

Finally, if a Rotte or Schwarm was attacked from behind, a quick turn by the formation would see the attacker immediately come under threat himself. If the rear section of an RAF formation was bounced, the aircraft under attack had usually been shot down well before another pilot could attempt to fend off the enemy fighters.

In the 'vic', only the leader searched for the enemy, as his two wingmen had to concentrate on remaining in tight formation. This left them highly susceptible to attack from behind and below, and this blind spot was repeatedly exploited by the Jagdwaffe in the opening days and months of the battle. Indeed, if the rear section of an RAF formation was bounced, the aircraft under attack had usually been shot down well before another pilot could attempt to fend off the enemy fighters.

The futility of these formations, and the FAA, were brought home to the Spitfire squadrons in their first engagements over Dunkirk. Al Deere was lucky to escape with his life when No. 54 Sqn tried to carry out such an attack on He 111s over the French coast on 24 May 1940:

The squadron had not been on patrol very long before Flt Lt Max Pearson's voice screeched over the R/T, 'Tally ho, Tally ho, enemy aircraft above and ahead.' About 3,000ft above us, and clearly silhouetted against a blue sky, a large formation of German bombers ploughed westwards towards Dunkirk unmolested and apparently unprotected. 'Sitting ducks,' I thought.

On the eve of the Battle of Britain, Fighter Command ordered its units to loosen their Battle Formations and have the last section weave in order to cover the squadron's rear. This change did little to negate the Jagdwaffe's superior tactics, and resulted in heavy casualties amongst the exposed 'weavers'.

'Hornet squadron, full throttle, climbing to attack', came the order from Flt Lt 'Prof' Leathart, who was leading the squadron. 'Hornet squadron, No. 5 attack, No. 5 attack, GO.'

Simultaneously, the sections fanned out into the various echelons necessary for this type of attack, and as they did so individual pilots selected a particular bomber target. But we had reckoned without interference from fighter escort – after all, no consideration

ENGAGING THE ENEMY

In 1940, most fighters had enough ammunition for 12 to 15 seconds' worth of fighting, so the pilot had to be selective about what he chose to fire at, and when, with a careful judgement of distance and angle. Most decisive fighter encounters ended within a few seconds of the attack commencing. One aircraft dived on another from behind or out of the sun ('Beware the Hun in the Sun' was a common adage in the RAF), opened fire for two or three seconds and then broke away – a classic aerial ambush known as the 'bounce'. However, if neither side had an initial advantage, then the fighters would 'dogfight' – the aim being to get on the opponent's tail – hence the name. Speed and manoeuvrability were crucial in such an instance, with the tighter the turn, the greater the ability to get behind an opponent.

Robert Bungay in his book *The Most Dangerous Enemy* identified four key factors. The first factor was the pilot's ability to exploit his aircraft's performance to the maximum. Secondly, excellent eyesight was necessary, a skill some pilots sought to improve upon. 'Sailor' Malan used to fix on a dot on a wall, look away and then turn his head and see how quickly he could focus on it again. Bob Doe used to search the sky systematically, dividing his view into four separate quarters with an emphasis on peripheral vision. You also had to be a good shot. Early experience with shotguns

often characterized the famous aces. Malan grew up on a farm in South Africa and began shooting when he was a boy. The great German ace Adolf Galland had been taken on his first hunting trip when he was just five. And of course they all needed a certain mental ability – the courage to know how to overcome fear and attack aggressively. For those that succeeded in aerial combat, it was a life-changing experience.

This illustration shows the Barr and Stroud GM 2 reflector unit which replaced the ring and bead sight in the Spitfire I from 1939 onwards. With the reflector gunsight in position and switched on, the pilot would see a white dot surrounded by a ring reflected onto his windscreen. Small rearview mirrors, similar to those in cars, were fixed above the windscreen to improve the view behind.

had been given to it in designing this type of attack, and our peacetime training had not envisaged interference from escort fighters. Experience is dearly bought.

'Christ, Messerschmitts – BREAK, BREAK.'

There was no need for a second warning. At the word 'Break', and with one accord, the squadron split in all directions, all thoughts of blazing enemy bombers ousted by the desire to survive.

Somehow, No. 54 Sqn suffered no losses to the attacking Bf 109Es, its pilots instead claiming nine German fighters destroyed – a testament to the skill of the pilots if not the original tactics. Such tactics were questioned by the pilots once back at their Hornchurch base. Plt Off Colin Gray, who like Al Deere was a Kiwi, and would also become a leading Spitfire ace, having had his aircraft turned upside down by an exploding cannon shell commented:

From behind me, I felt them. In future, I've no intention of offering myself as a target to Hun fighters while the rest of the squadron disappears in all directions other than that in which some unfortunate like me is getting hell beaten out of him.

Although No. 54 Sqn vowed there and then to abandon FAAs, however, 'vic' formations would continue well into 1941 until falling out of practice. Indeed, officially, pilots were forbidden from implementing new tactics at unit level. In reality there was no actual time available for Fighter Command to rectify this problem through the issuing of new tactics on the eve of the Battle of Britain. Future ace Plt Off Bobby Oxpsring, who was flying Spitfires with No. 66 Sqn at the time, explained the predicament facing frontline pilots at the time:

We knew that there was a lot wrong with our tactics during the Battle of Britain, but it was one hell of a time to alter everything we had practised. We had not time to experiment when we were in combat three or four times a day. Moreover, we were getting fresh pilots straight out of flying schools who were trained, barely, to use the old type of close formation – they simply could not have coped with something radically different.

In an effort to improve the operability of the 'vic', Fighter Command permitted squadrons to widen out the formations, thus allowing pilots to search the skies for the enemy more freely, rather than concentrating on close formation keeping with the lead fighter. A section or pair of aircraft would also now fly as 'weavers' some 1,000ft above and behind the main formation in an effort to prevent surprise attacks from the rear – without anyone to protect their tails, countless 'weavers' were duly shot down during the Battle of Britain. These modifications certainly improved the search and mutual support capabilities of Fighter Command's formations, but did nothing to improve their ability to perform tight turns without losing cohesion.

A number of squadrons that had seen action over Dunkirk began to modify their tactics. Amongst these was No. 74 Sqn, which included the great tactician Flt Lt 'Sailor' Malan within its ranks. During the closing stages of the battle, Malan divided his aircraft

into three sections of four. If the formation broke up, Spitfires would then become fighting pairs. Clearly, combat experience and some amount of 'bending of the rules' ensured survival. He, along with Al Deere and Bob Stanford Tuck, also began to question the gun harmonization distances of their Spitfires. The official thinking pre-war had been to fill the air with 0.303-in. bullets at a distance of 400 yards ahead of the line of flight. However, following combat experience, Malan was adamant that the distance should be reduced to 250 yards, thus forcing pilots to get in close to their targets so that one could not miss. This change was finally officially sanctioned in the summer of 1940.

At about the same time as this change was made, Spitfires also began to be armed with a new kind of incendiary round known to pilots as De Wilde ammunition. Unlike the standard incendiary ammunition in use at the start of the war, De Wilde had no flame or smoke trace. However, it did produce a small flash on impact with the target, thus for the first time providing pilots with the confirmation that their aim was good.

Despite initially inferior tactics, the sheer ability of Fighter Command's pilots, combined with the superb command-and-control network and the combat performance of the Spitfire and, to a lesser degree, the Hurricane in combat, allowed the RAF to retain air supremacy over the UK.

A Schwarm of Bf 109Es heads for England in the late summer of 1940. The aircraft have closed up for the benefit of the camera in this shot, as normally they would have been well spaced in 'finger four' formation. The Schwarm would then fly as two Rotten, or loose pairs, with 200m of separation between each aircraft. This formation was far better suited to the fighter-versus-fighter combat that predominated from May to December 1940.

GERMAN TACTICS

The German fighter force that engaged the RAF during 1940 was by far the most experienced and tactically advanced anywhere in the world at that time. Although less than a third of its pilots had seen action in Spain, the lessons learned there had been introduced throughout the Jadgwaffe. Werner Mölders was the most influential of all Condor Legion veterans, and what he had learned fighting Spanish Nationalist aircraft was officially institutionalized in training in the lead up to World War II.

His philosophy for success in combat saw the emphasis placed more on fighting than flying. Experience had taught Mölders that the best way to achieve this was to abandon the three-aircraft 'vic' and go with the two-aircraft *Rotte* (pair), which in turn formed the basic fighting unit for all Jagdwaffe formations. Within the pair, the *Rottenführer* (pair leader) was responsible for making the kills and his wingman (the *Katschmarek*) protected the leader's tail. The wingman did not worry about where he was flying, or what to do next – he simply had to follow his leader. He usually held position some 200 yards away from the Rottenführer, flying almost in line abreast formation. Each pilot concentrated his search of the sky inwards, so as to cover his partner's blind spot.

Two Rotten made up a *Schwarm* (flight), flying some 300 yards apart – roughly the turning radius of a Bf 109E at combat speed. The leading Rotte typically flew to one side and slightly ahead of the other, and a Staffel formation comprised three Schwarme either stepped up in line astern or in line abreast. The Jadgwaffe also devised the 'cross-over turn' to avoid aircraft on the outside of a Schwarm becoming stragglers when the formation turned at high cruising speed in an area where contact with the enemy was likely. Each pilot held his speed going into the turn and the Rotte simply changed position in the formation during the manoeuvre.

During the early stages of World War II, the Bf 109E enjoyed a superior altitude performance to all the fighters it came up against, so the favoured tactic of the Jagdwaffe was to get above their opponents and attempt to bounce them, if possible using the sun to mask their approach. After a single firing pass, the Jagdflieger would use the speed gained in their diving attack to climb back up into a position from which to perform any repeat attacks. With enemy fighters usually being slower and more manoeuvrable, German pilots tried to avoid turning dogfights wherever possible.

If bounced, the Rotte or Schwarm would typically turn individually to meet the attack, and if there was no time for this, they would take advantage of the direct injection system fitted to their Bf 109Es by bunting over into a dive. The *Abschwung* (American 'Split-S') was also used as an alternative escape route, the pilot performing a half-roll pulled through into a steep dive at full throttle – this manoeuvre could only be done with plenty of altitude in hand, as up to 15,000ft in height would be lost.

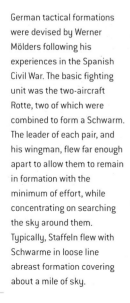

German tactical formations were devised by Werner Mölders following his experiences in the Spanish Civil War. The basic fighting unit was the two-aircraft Rotte, two of which were combined to form a Schwarm. The leader of each pair, and his wingman, flew far enough apart to allow them to remain in formation with the minimum of effort, while concentrating on searching the sky around them. Typically, Staffeln flew with Schwarme in loose line abreast formation covering about a mile of sky.

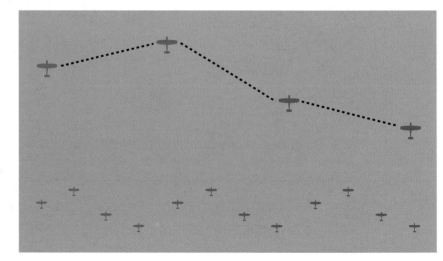

These formations and tactics served the Jagdwaffe well over Dunkirk and for much of the Battle of Britain, with Rottenführer having just one job to do – find and destroy the enemy. When they were found, the formation leader was the one who went in for the kill, leaving his wingmen to cover his tail. By sticking to the Freie Jagd tactic, pilots of the calibre of Mölders, Galland, Ihlefeld, Oesau and Wick all racked up impressive scores. Lesser-known pilots were also well served by these tactics, including 3./JG 52's Oberleutnant Ulrich Steinhilper on 26 September 1940:

We were approaching Dover when we saw a whole squadron of Spitfires spread out in line astern below us, with a weaver on either side at the back. They were so well defined against the blue-green of the sea that we couldn't have missed them. My *Staffelführer*, Oberleutnant Helmut Kühle, instructed me to take one of the weavers and he said that he'd take care of the other. When the rest of the squadron saw that this had been accomplished, they could then pick their own targets. These were good tactics, as the weavers were there to protect the rear of the flight, and if they could be taken out without raising the alarm, there would be a good chance of the rest of the squadron bagging the majority of the enemy aircraft. This was what was so foolish about flying this kind of formation.

We peeled away and I began to position my fighter. The red ring of the Revi gunsight was projected onto the windscreen, and I'd already flipped over the trigger for both the nose guns and the wing cannon, ready for the attack. Gradually, the Spitfire filled the ring of the sight and I increased the pressure on the triggers. Four lines of tracer hosed out towards the target and I saw strikes, the aircraft spinning away. Instead of chasing it down, I altered course slightly and went for the next Spitfire in line. Again I saw hits before I broke away to safety.

Sitting forlornly on its belly at Winchet Hill, near Marden in Kent, this Bf 109E-4 of Stab II./JG 3 was brought down by future ace Plt Off Basil 'Stapme' Stapleton of No. 603 Sqn on 5 September 1940. Its pilot, Oberleutnant Franz von Werra, who was already an ace, later gained fame as the 'One That Got Away' – he was the only German prisoner of war to escape British captivity, fleeing from Canada to the neutral USA and then being smuggled back to Germany in 1941.

As the Battle of Britain progressed, however, the tactical advantage enjoyed by the Jagdwaffe was steadily eroded by the unbreakable spirit of Fighter Command, its radar coverage of the Channel and its efficient fighter control system. The Bf 109E's short range also became more of a problem as the Kampfgeschwader started to go after targets farther inland from the south coast. Oberstleutnant Adolf Galland, Geschwaderkommodore of JG 26 by the end of the Battle of Britain, wrote at length about this problem in his autobiography *The First and the Last*, stating that the Messerschmitt fighter's lack of range was critical to the outcome of the Battle of Britain:

It used to take us roughly half an hour from take-off to crossing the English coast at the narrowest point of the Channel. Having a tactical flying time of about 80 minutes in the Bf 109E, we therefore had about 20 minutes to complete our task. This fact limited the distance of penetration, German fighter squadrons based on the Pas de Calais and on the Contentin peninsula barely being able to cover the south-eastern part of England. Circles drawn from these two bases at an operational range of 125 miles overlapped approximately in the London area. Everything beyond was practically out of our reach. An operating radius of 125 miles was sufficient for local defence, but not enough for such tasks as bomber escort, which were now being demanded of us.

It was assumed that the appearance of German fighter squadrons over England would draw the British fighters into the area within our range, where they would be destroyed, beaten, or at least decimated in large-scale air battles. Things turned out differently. Our fighter formations took off. The first air battles took place as expected and according to plan. Due to the German superiority, these attacks, had they been continued, would certainly have achieved the attempted goal, but the RAF fighters were recalled from this area long before this goal was achieved.

The weakened squadrons left their bases near the coast and used them only for emergency landings or to refuel and rearm. They were concentrated in a belt around London in readiness for our bomber attacks. Thus they evaded the attack *in* the air in order to encounter more effectively the attack *from*

Trademark cigar in his left hand, Major Adolf Galland, clothed in a captured RAF Bomber Command Irvin sheepskin flying suit, was a leading Spitfire I/II killer in 1940–41. Flying with JG 27 and then JG 26, he claimed 25 Supermarine fighters destroyed. Galland survived the war with 104 victories to his credit.

the air, which would logically follow. The German fighters found themselves in a similar predicament to a dog on a chain who wants to attack the foe but cannot harm him because of the limitations of the chain.

As losses to both German fighters and bombers mounted, and Fighter Command's resolve seemingly remained intact, senior officers in the Luftwaffe sought to lay the blame at the feet of the Jagdgeschwader, as Galland recalled:

> We had the impression that, whatever we did, we were bound to be wrong. Fighter protection for bombers created many problems which had to be solved in action. Bomber pilots preferred close screening in which their formation was surrounded by pairs of fighters pursuing a zigzag course. Obviously, the visible presence of the protective fighters gave the bomber pilots a greater sense of security. However, this was a faulty conclusion, because a fighter can only carry out this purely defensive task by taking the initiative in the offensive. He must never wait until attacked because he then loses the chance of acting.
>
> We fighter pilots certainly preferred the 'free chase during the approach and over the target area'. This in fact gives the greatest relief and the best protection for the bomber force, although not perhaps a sense of security for the latter.

Reichsmarschall Göring, however, did not side with Jagdflieger when it came to allowing them to continue to wage the Battle of Britain on their terms. Indeed, in late August he ordered that all Jagdgeschwader were to remain close to the bombers that they were escorting, and on no account were they to engage enemy fighters unless they or their bombers came under a direct threat of attack. With the bombers cruising

Bf 109E-4 'White 10' of 1./JG 2 taxies out from its dispersal point at Beaumont-le-Roger, in Normandy, in early September 1940. This unit regularly diced with Spitfire and Hurricane squadrons based in No. 10 Group, defending south-west England. As this photograph clearly shows, forward visibility for the pilot over the nose was virtually non-existent thanks to the fighter's DB 601 engine.

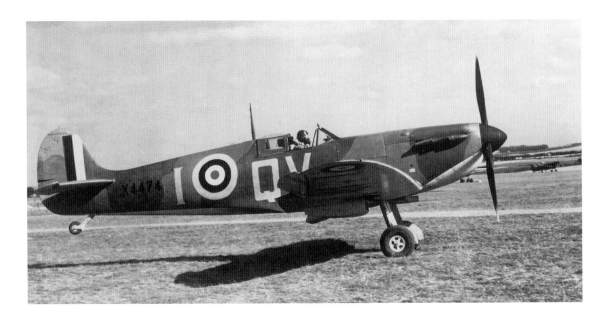

Spitfire IA X4474 of No. 19 Sqn, with Sgt Bernard Jennings at the controls, scrambles from Fowlmere, in Cambridgeshire, in late September 1940. On the 27th of that month, Jennings and X4474 were credited with downing a Bf 109E south of the Thames – No. 19 Sqn claimed eight Emils destroyed during this engagement. No. 19 Sqn claimed 60.5 victories, although only 26 of these could be matched up with known German losses.

at a much slower speed than the fighters, the Jagdflieger had to weave in order to maintain station, and yet still retain a high cruising speed in the combat area. By ordering the Jagdwaffe to fly close-formation missions, Göring totally nullified the effectiveness of the previously superior German fighter tactics, thus surrendering the initiative in the skies over southern England to the RAF.

Losses amongst the Bf 109E Geschwader rose steeply once they were 'chained' to the bomber formations, and one of those men shot down was six-victory ace Feldwebel Heinrich Hoehnisch of 1./JG 53.

On my last mission, on 9 September 1940, our task was to give direct fighter cover to the rear of an He 111 bomber formation. One *Kette* [three aircraft in a 'vic' formation] of bombers got separated, so our Staffel looked after them. We had only seven Bf 109s, and I was tail-end Charlie with Oberfeldwebel Mueller. Approaching London Docks, there was no contact with the enemy, but I was sure that we could expect attacks out of the sun as soon as we turned 180 degrees for our return flight. To my surprise, I saw, when I was looking towards the rest of my Staffel, six Spitfires on a reciprocal course in line astern about 50 metres above me. To avoid the inevitable attack, I tried to come up with my Staffel flying in front and below me. When I was level with my Staffelkapitän, I thought I had made it.

However, there was a rattle like an explosion in my aeroplane and, with the pressure of a blowtorch, flames hit my face. With the greatest difficulty, I got out of my aeroplane. I landed with severe burns to my face and bullet wounds to my right calf. I stayed in the hospital in Woolwich for two months. (Goss, *The Luftwaffe Fighters' Battle of Britain*)

Hoehnisch had been shot down by No. 19 Sqn Spitfire ace Flt Lt Wilf Clouston in an engagement that had lasted just a matter of seconds, a typical example of the Spitfire-versus-Bf 109E clashes that occurred throughout the Battle of Britain.

STATISTICS AND ANALYSIS

Bf 109Es and Spitfires fought each other from 23 May 1940, when No. 54 Sqn engaged aircraft from I./JG 27 near Dunkirk, to 21 December 1940, when No. 92 Sqn downed a Bf 109E-4 of 7.(F)/LG 2 over Dungeness. The two types continued to engage in mortal combat well into 1941 too.

Fighter Command (and No. 11 Group in particular) had done its best throughout 1940 to send its 19 Spitfire squadrons up against the Jagdwaffe's eight Jagdgeschwader, leaving units equipped with slower, less capable Hurricanes to engage the bombers. Of course both RAF types would end up 'mixing it' with Bf 109Es on a daily basis, and Spitfire pilots also downed their fair share of bombers. Nevertheless, a large proportion of the aircraft claimed destroyed by Spitfire pilots, and aces in particular, were Bf 109Es, and the same applied to the Jagdwaffe.

Fighter Command suffered significant Spitfire losses in 1940, with 72 (nearly one-third of its frontline strength of these aircraft at this time) being lost during operations to cover the evacuation of Dunkirk. August 1940 would prove to be the worst month for Spitfire losses, with 136 fighters destroyed. Overall, during the four months of the Battle of Britain, 361 Spitfires were lost and a further 352 damaged. Fortunately for Fighter Command, and the free world, production of the aircraft far outstripped attrition, with 747 Spitfire I/IIs being delivered in the summer and autumn of 1940.

During this same period, the Jagdwaffe lost 610 Bf 109Es, which compares favourably to Fighter Command's 1,023 Spitfires and Hurricanes. Of course, the only targets presented to the Jagdflieger during this period were fighters, and it appears that they claimed around 770 of the aircraft lost by Fighter Command. This gave the

Bf 109E pilots a favourable kill ratio of 1.2:1, but this was nowhere near the 5:1 target that Oberst Theo Osterkamp (Jagdfliegerführer 2) had set his pilots in July in order to achieve the desired air superiority required for *Sea Lion*.

As the campaign ground on, the Jagdwaffe, like Fighter Command, also began to see its pilot numbers decrease, although production of Bf 109Es kept ahead of losses with an average of 155 being delivered per month. Some 906 Emil pilots were deemed to be operational in July, and this number had fallen to 735 by September.

Both sides certainly enjoyed significant aerial successes during the course of the Battle of Britain, but the overclaiming of victories was rife in both the Jagdwaffe and Fighter Command. For example, the 19 Spitfire units claimed 1,064.5 victories between 1 July and 31 October, but exhaustive research by historian John Alcorn (published in the September 1996 issue of *Aeroplane Monthly* magazine) has shown that only 521.49 of these claims can be substantiated – an average of 27 kills per squadron – a result no doubt, of the confusion of aerial combat. The accuracy of these figures is borne out by the fact that the Luftwaffe lost 1,218 aircraft in total to fighter attacks during this period.

Of the ten top-scoring units by substantiated claims, six flew Spitfires, and two of these squadrons proved to be Bf 109E killers to boot as per the No. 11 Group strategy. No. 603 Sqn topped the list with 57.8 kills (from 67 originally claimed), with 47 of these being Bf 109Es, and No. 41 Sqn, which was third on the list, was credited with 45.3 kills (from 89.5 claimed), of which 33.5 were Emils. Unsurprisingly, the two leading Spitfire aces of 1940, Flg Off Brian Carbury and Plt Off Eric Lock, both of whom were credited with 15 Bf 109E victories apiece, served with these units in 1940.

German kill claims were, if anything, even more wildly optimistic than those of Fighter Command, leading senior Luftwaffe officers to believe that the RAF was

Having just claimed his 21st kill (a Hurricane), Oberfeldwebel Werner Machold of 1./JG 2 smiles for the camera as he looks at the new victory bar applied to the rudder of his Bf 109E on 4 September 1940. Machold would claim 13 Spitfire I/IIs destroyed between 26 May 1940 and 19 May 1941. Hit by anti-aircraft fire whilst attacking a convoy off Portland on 9 June 1941, Machold force-landed his Bf 109E-7/Z near Swanage, in Dorset, and was captured. His score stood at 32 victories at the time of his imprisonment.

literally on its knees – this, of course, was not the case. The post-war comparison of German kill claims with RAF losses shows that very few match up! This was partly the result of the inherent confusion associated with air combat – a number of pilots often claimed the same victim. Overclaiming was also to be expected when the Luftwaffe's system of medals, promotion and profile was closely linked to a pilot's score. It was also virtually impossible to confirm a kill by the examination of wreckage, as most Spitfires and Hurricanes fell either on British soil or in the Channel.

The German tactical system was geared up for a chosen few to claim the bulk of the kills, with the rest supporting – and protecting – them, often with their lives. The victory and attrition figures for JG 51 prove just that, its statistics being typical for most of the Jagdgeschwader in 1940. The unit lost ten pilots in July of that year, half of which had failed to score a single kill prior to their demise. The remaining five had claimed just 11 between them. This ratio was to remain remarkably constant through to June 1941, when the unit headed east for the invasion of the USSR.

Just over half of the 100 pilots lost by JG 51 during this time had not claimed a single victory, and of the rest, 35 had fewer than five kills. Aerial combat in 1940–41 was 'natural selection' at its harshest, and if a new pilot survived his first few missions, his chances of survival were significantly improved, at least in the short to medium term.

At the other end of the scale, 16 *experten* who claimed at least five Spitfire I/IIs destroyed scored some or all of their victories flying with JG 51 during this period. Leading the pack was Hauptmann Walter Oesau, who claimed 26 Spitfire I/IIs whilst flying with III./JG 51. Oberleutnant Hermann-Friedrich Joppien (13 kills), Major Werner Mölders (ten kills) and Hauptmann Ernst Wiggers (ten kills) were the other pilots to achieve Spitfire victories in double figures in 1940–41, although the latter was killed in action by a Hurricane pilot on 11 September 1940.

At the end of the day the Battle of Britain provided the Allies with their first victory in World War II. Although the Bf 109E Jagdgeschwader more than held their own,

Unlike most of the leading RAF aces of 1940, Plt Off Eric Lock had not served with Fighter Command pre-war. Indeed, he had been posted to No. 41 Sqn after completing his flying training in early August 1940. A gutsy dogfighter, Lock would claim 26 victories between 15 August 1940 and 14 July 1941. His tally of 15 Bf 109Es destroyed equals the score attained by that other great Emil killer, Flg Off Brian Carbury. Lock was posted missing in action during a fighter sweep over France with No. 611 Sqn on 3 August 1941.

despite operating at the very limit of their range, the seemingly invincible Luftwaffe had been comprehensively beaten. However, Fighter Command had emerged from the 123-day campaign stronger than it had gone into it, despite losing 1,023 fighters and having 515 pilots killed. It would then eventually move onto the offensive as the threat of invasion of Britain ebbed away.

LEADING SPITFIRE MK I/II Bf 109E KILLERS 1940–41

	Bf 109E Kills	Final Score	Unit
Flg Off Brian Carbury	15	15 (+2sh)	No. 603 Sqn
Plt Off Eric Lock	15	26	No. 41 Sqn
Plt Off Colin Gray	12	27 (+2sh)	No. 54 Sqn
Flg Off Pat Hughes	12	14 (+3sh)	No. 234 Sqn
Sgt William Franklin	11	13 (+3sh)	No. 65 Sqn
Flg Off Des McMullen	10.5	17 (+5sh)	Nos 54 and 222 Sqns
Flg Off John Webster	9.5	11 (+2sh)	No. 41 Sqn
Sqn Ldr John Ellis	9	13 (+1sh)	No. 610 Sqn
Sqn Ldr Adolf Malan	9	27 (+7sh)	No. 74 Sqn
Flt Sgt George Unwin	8.5	13 (+2sh)	No. 19 Sqn

LEADING Bf 109E SPITFIRE I/II KILLERS 1940–41

	Kills	Final Score	Unit
Hptm Herbert Ihlefeld	33	132	Stab I.(J)/LG 2, 2.(J)/LG 2 and 2.(J)/LG 2
Hptm Walter Oesau	26	127	7./JG 51 and Stab III./JG 51
Maj Adolf Galland	25	104	Stab JG 27, Stab III./JG 26 and Stab JG 26
Maj Helmut Wick	24	56	3./JG 2, Stab I./JG 2 and Stab JG 2
Ltn Erich Schmidt	15	47	9./JG 53
Oblt Hermann-Friedrich Joppien	13	70	1./JG 51
Oblt Werner Machold	13	32	9./JG 2 & 9./JG 2
Maj Werner Mölders	13	115	III./JG 53 and Stab JG 51
Oblt Josef Priller	13	101	6./JG 51 and 1./JG 26
Hptm Gerhard Schöpfel	13	45	9./JG 26 and III./JG 26
Ltn Horst Ulenberg	13	16	2./JG 26
Ltn Friedrich Geisshardt	12	102	1.(J)/LG 2 and 2.(J)/LG 2
Oblt Hans Hahn	12	108	4./JG 2
Oblt Gustav Rödel	12	98	4./JG 27
Oblt Hans-Ekkhard Bob	10	60	9./JG 54, 7./JG 54 and Stab III./JG 54
Hptm Ernst Wiggers	10	13	2./JG 51

AFTERMATH

Officially, the Battle of Britain ended for the RAF on 31 October 1940. However, both Fighter Command and the Jagdwaffe continued to lock horns regularly until the end of the year. Indeed, on 1 November four Biggin Hill-based Spitfires were shot down by Bf 109Es from JG 26 that were escorting Ju 87s sent to attack a convoy off Dover – the kind of attack that had signalled the start of the Battle of Britain four months earlier! This particular raid was unusual for the period, as the Luftwaffe had by then reassigned the majority of its dedicated bomber units to night raids, using high-flying Bf 109E Jabos to attack targets in the south-east during daylight hours.

These raids were carried out at altitudes of between 26,000ft and 33,000ft, and at high speeds, presenting Fighter Command with little chance to intercept them. Fortunately, the bombloads carried by the Jabos was small, and accuracy of the weapons released from 18,000ft was generally poor. Nevertheless, Jabo attacks by Emils would continue well into 1941.

By then the Bf 109E's days as the premier German fighter

Sqn Ldr 'Sailor' Malan's loose line-astern formation now possessed mutual support, coverage of blind spots to the rear and cohesion if forced to turn in combat. It was also much easier to fly.

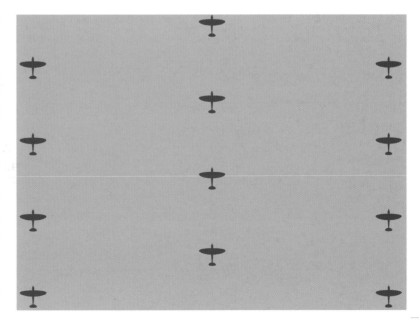

on the Channel front were well and truly numbered. As early as 9 October 1940, Major Werner Mölders, Geschwaderkommodore of JG 51, had flown his first combat sortie over southern England in the Emil's successor, the Bf 109F. Over coming months, the improved 'Friedrich' would be issued to JG 53, JG 3, JG 2 and JG 26, in that order. The last frontline Emils on the Channel front, flown by the latter unit's II Gruppe, were still 'mixing it' with the RAF's Spitfires and Hurricanes over France as late as 7 September 1941, after which they were replaced by the all-new Fw 190A-1.

The RAF, meanwhile, had gone from being on the defensive in 1940 to taking the fight to the Germans in 1941. In the vanguard of this campaign was Fighter Command, whose new commander-in-chief, Chief Marshal Sir Sholto Douglas, wanted his squadrons 'leaning forward into France'. The first such mission had actually been performed by two pilots from Spitfire-equipped No. 66 Sqn on 20 December 1940, when they strafed Le Touquet. This was the first time Spitfires had sortied over France since the fall of Dunkirk. Large-scale operations aimed at enticing the Jagdwaffe into combat over France and the Low Countries commenced in earnest in January 1941, with the first 'Circus' mission taking place on the 10th of that month. Spitfire units from Nos 10 and 11 Groups were heavily involved in this long-running offensive from the very start, escorting medium bombers sent to attack various military targets in occupied Europe.

More and more Hurricane units now switched to Spitfires – often battle-tired Mk Is, but also newer Mk IIs and the significantly improved Mk V. And with operations progressing ever deeper into occupied Europe, the short-ranged Spitfire was finding it difficult to offer the vulnerable medium bombers the protection they required. In a desperate effort to stretch the endurance of the Supermarine fighter, 60 Spitfire IIs were built with a fixed 40-gal tank fitted under the port wing. Designated the Spitfire II Long Range, these aircraft saw considerable service from the spring of 1941 onwards. Despite being built in only modest numbers, the Spitfire II (LR)s flew with no fewer than eight units, as aircraft were passed between squadrons rotating in and out of No. 11 Group.

By then the tactics being employed by Spitfire squadrons in the front line had also altered dramatically from those in place for much of the Battle of Britain. Several units had taken it upon themselves to modify the formations they flew when going into combat, and at the forefront of these changes was Spitfire-equipped No. 74 Sqn. Its CO, Sqn Ldr 'Sailor' Malan, was effectively the Werner Mölders of Fighter Command, being one of the best tacticians in the RAF. He had also claimed nine Bf 109Es destroyed during 1940, so his theories on fighter formations had been formulated through bitter combat experiences.

During the final stages of the Battle of Britain, Malan began dividing his 12-aircraft formations into three sections of four, rather than the traditional four sections of three in an unwieldy 'vic'. Now, if a formation of Spitfires broke up after being bounced, its four-aircraft sections would split into two fighting pairs, which operated similarly to the German Rotte. With the three section leaders flying in a widely-spaced 'V',

and the rest of their sections in line astern behind them, Malan's formation now possessed mutual support, coverage of blind spots to the rear and cohesion if forced to turn in combat. The loose line-astern formation was also much easier to fly than tight 'Battle Formation', thus freeing pilots to devote most of their time looking out for the enemy, rather than watching what their section leader was up to. Malan's new formation was soon officially implemented throughout Fighter Command, as was the German 'finger four' Schwarm.

Virtually all Spitfire I/IIs had either been relegated to Training Command or rebuilt as Mk VBs by December 1941, and, fittingly, veteran Battle of Britain unit No. 152 Sqn had the honour of flying the final sweeps over enemy territory in these early mark fighters the following month. Later marks of Spitfire would, of course, continue to take the fight to the Jagdwaffe, duelling with improved versions of the Bf 109 to help the Allies ultimately claim final victory in Europe in World War II.

The importance of the victory of the Battle of Britain, and the success that the Spitfire pilots achieved cannot be overstated. It was the first victory secured by the Allies against the Third Reich and it was a necessary victory to ensure later successes. Without victory here the Battle of the Atlantic could not have been fought, it is doubtful whether America would have been convinced to enter the European conflict, and Britain could not have fulfilled her final destiny as a staging ground for the D-Day invasion force of June 1944. Like Stalingrad, the Battle of Britain was one of the true turning points of the war, but one that was achieved without costing millions of lives. Indeed, as Churchill so famously concluded, 'Never was so much owed by so many to so few.'

No. 72 Sqn Spitfire IIAs form up off the Kent coast in the summer of 1941 prior to heading across the Channel on yet another 'Circus' over France. The unit is still operating in 'vics' of three here, although the aircraft have closed up specially for the photographer, strapped into a Blenheim bomber.

FURTHER READING

Books

Bungay, S., *The Most Dangerous Enemy* (Aurum, 2000)

Caldwell, D.J., *The JG 26 War Diary Vol 1.* (Grub Street, 1998)

Cossey, B., *A Tiger's Tale* (J&KH, 2002)

Cull, B., Lander, B. with Weiss, H. *Twelve Days in May* (Grub Street, 1995)

Deere, A., *Nine Lives* (Wingham Press, 1991)

Deighton, L., *Fighter* (Book Club Associates, 1978)

Doe, B., *Fighter Pilot* (CCB, 2004)

Ekkehard-Bob, H., *Betrayed Ideals* (Cerberus, 2004)

Fernandez-Sommerau, *Messerschmitt Bf 109 Recognition Manual* (Classic Publications, 2004)

Foreman, J., *Battle of Britain – The Forgotten Months* (Air Research Publications, 1988)

Franks, N., *RAF Fighter Command Losses of the Second World War* (Midland Publishing Ltd, 1997)

Franks, N., *Air Battle Dunkirk* (Grub Street, 2000)

Franks, N., *Sky Tiger* (Crécy, 1994)

Galland, A., *The First and the Last* (Fontana, 1971)

Goss, C., *The Luftwaffe Fighters' Battle of Britain* (Crécy, 2000)

Green, W., *Warplanes of the Third Reich* (Doubleday, 1972)

van Ishoven, A., *Messerschmitt Bf 109 at War* (Ian Allan, 1977)

Jefford, C. G., *RAF Squadrons* (Airlife, 2001)

Ketley, B. and Rolfe, M., *Luftwaffe Fledglings 1935–1945* (Hikoki Publications, 1996)

Lake, J., *The Battle of Britain* (Silverdale Books, 2000)

Matusiak, W., *Polish Wings 6 - Supermarine Spitfire I/II* (Stratus, 2007)

Mombeek, E., with Smith, J.R., and Creek,E., *Jagdwaffe Volume 1 Section 2 – Spanish Civil War* (Classic Publications, 1999)

Mombeek, E., with Wadman, D. and Creek, E., *Jagdwaffe Volume 2 Section 1 – Battle of Britain Phase One* (Classic Publications, 2001)

Mombeek, E., with Wadman, D., and Pegg, M., *Jagdwaffe Volume 2 Section 2 – Battle of Britain Phase Two* (Classic Publications, 2001)

Mombeek, E., with Wadman, D. and Pegg, M., *Jagdwaffe Volume 2 Section 3 – Battle of Britain Phase Three* (Classic Publications, 2002)

Mombeek, E., with Wadman, D., and Pegg, M., *Jagdwaffe Volume 2 Section 4 – Battle of Britain Phase Four* (Classic Publications, 2002)

Morgan, E., and Shacklady, E., *Spitfire – The History* (Key Publishing, 1993)

Obermaier, E., *Die Ritterkreuzträger der Luftwaffe Jagdflieger 1939–1945* (Verlag Dieter Hoffmann, 1966)

Price, Dr A., *Luftwaffe Handbook 1939–1945* (Ian Allan, 1976)

Price, Dr A., *Spitfire – A Complete Fighting History* (Promotional Reprint Company, 1991)

Price, Dr A., *World War II Fighter Conflict* (Purnell, 1975)

Price, Dr A., Aircraft of the Aces 12 *Spitfire Mark I/II Aces 1939–41* (Osprey, 1996)

Ramsey, W., (ed.), *The Battle of Britain Then and Now Mk IV* (After The Battle, 1987)

Ross, D., Blanche, B. and Simpson, W., *The Greatest Squadron of Them All, Volume 1* (Grub Street, 2003)

Shores, C., and Williams, C., *Aces High* (Grub Street, 1994)

Steinhilper, U., and Osborne, P., *Spitfire On My Tail* (Independent Books, 1989)

Sturtivant, R., *The History of Britain's Military Training Aircraft* (Haynes, 1987)

Terbeck, H., van der Meer, H., and Sturtivant, R., *Spitfire International* (Air-Britain, 2002)

Townsend, P., *Duel of Eagles* (Weidenfeld, 1990)

Wilson, S., *Spitfire* (Aerospace Publications, 1999)

Magazines

Alcorn, J., 'B of B Top Guns', *Aeroplane Monthly* (September 1996): p.14–18

Donald, David, 'Messerschmitt Bf 109: The First Generation', Wings of Fame Volume 4: p.38–77

Price, Dr A., 'Database – Spitfire Prototype & Mark I', *Aeroplane (*March 2006): p. 39–62

Websites

Tony Wood's Combat Claims and Casualties – www.lesbutler.ip3.co.uk/tony/tony wood.htm

Aces of the Luftwaffe – www.luftwaffe.cz

INDEX